MUMBAI
HOUSING COMPASS 2.0

VOLUME 2

Analysis of New Real Estate Launches

From 2020-2025

Rahul Ajmera

Dr. Adv. Harshul Savla D.Litt.

notionpress.com

INDIA • SINGAPORE • MALAYSIA

ISBN

Hardcase 979-8-90392-637-4
Paperback 979-8-90319-951-8

Contents

About the Author

Rahul Ajmera

Rahul Ajmera is a third-generation real estate developer and the driving force behind Vasupujya Corporation, a family-run enterprise with deep roots in Pune's real estate landscape since 1980. With their distinctive philosophy of "Quality over Quantity," Vasupujya Corporation has established a development approach that stands apart in today's mass-production real estate market—executing only one project at a time, on self-owned land parcels, with personal oversight throughout the construction process. Vasupujya Corporation has delivered over 1400 homes in 20+ projects spread over 10,00,000 square feet built-up area in Mumbai and Pune till date.

A Civil Engineering graduate from IIT Bombay, Rahul Ajmera made a strategic educational choice aligned with his family's real estate legacy. His professional background includes valuable work experience at industry giants - Shapoorji Pallonji and RBSA Advisors, providing him with a rare combination of engineering expertise and financial acumen that informs his data-driven development methodology.

Over the last decade, Rahul Ajmera has successfully overseen the delivery of multiple landmark projects across Pune, including Neco Beaumont at Mohammadwadi, Neco SkyPark at Pimple Nilakh, and Neco Alpha at Pimple Nilakh. Currently, the firm is developing Neco Park Central at Kharadi (Residential Units) and Neco Officers Ville near NIBM Road (NA Plots) - each project reflecting Rahul Ajmera's commitment to thoughtful design and practical living solutions.

What truly distinguishes Rahul Ajmera in Pune's competitive real estate sector is his pioneering use of data analytics to drive decision-making. Through his consultancy firm AREA Foresight, he provides critical market intelligence to real estate developers, financial institutions, and government bodies, helping them make informed decisions about property sizing and pricing. This analytical approach has established him as one of Pune's most reliable voices in real estate intelligence, with his market analyses and trend forecasts regularly featured across in newspapers and shared by prominent social media influencers.

Rahul Ajmera's commitment to transparency extends beyond his projects. Through myhomeinpune.com, he offers homebuyers unbiased information about real estate options in Pune without advertisement bias. His comprehensive HomeBuyer's Guide educates potential homeowners on critical aspects of property purchase, while his initiatives to organize bulk material purchases for CREDAI Pune Metro members help developers reduce construction costs.

A testament to Rahul Ajmera's client-focused philosophy is Vasupujya Corporation's post-possession engagement through regular community meetings and dedicated communication channels. "Our end goal isn't just building most homes, but building communities where most residents are happy," says Rahul, who regularly interacts with residents at his projects.

Beyond real estate, Rahul Ajmera has won several national and international accolades for Short Film Making during his college days at IIT Bombay. He also shares his travel and dining experiences online, bringing the same passion and attention to detail that characterizes his approach to real estate development.

Through his multifaceted contributions to Pune's real estate ecosystem, Rahul Ajmera represents a new generation of developers who combine technical expertise with market intelligence and customer-centricity—revolutionizing the industry one thoughtfully designed project at a time.

About the Author

Dr. Adv. Harshul Savla, D.Litt.

Dr. Harshul Savla, D.Litt. is Managing Partner of Suvidha Lifespaces which has successfully completed more than 2 million sq.ft. in last 35 years across Mumbai City under the able leadership of Mr. Pramesh Rambhiya. CRISIL India and Realty Icon Awards recognized Dr. Harshul as "Young Thought Leader" and Realty NXT featured him as "Young Turk of Real Estate Sector". He has won the prestigious CREDAI-MCHI Golden Pillar Award in the category of Best Debutant Real Estate Developer and has been awarded "Young Achiever of the Year" by CREDAI, ET NOW, CNN News 18, ZEE Business, MAHARASHTRA Times, ABP News, Realty+, MID DAY, Business World and Realty Quarter.

Dr. Harshul has featured in the Business World and Realty Plus "40 under 40" list as Real Estate's Young Turk consecutively in 2021, 2022, 2023, 2024 & 2025. He has also been awarded the prestigious "Pillars of Maharashtra" award in 2022 by Hon'ble Member of Parliament for Mumbai North. The Times Group's Economic Times has awarded Dr. Harshul Savla as an Inspiring Personality 2022 for exceptional contribution to Real Estate Sector. Mid Day's "Success Stories 2022" has featured Dr. Harshul's various achievements and journey. He has been a TEDx Speaker too.

Dr. Harshul has worked as EA to Ramesh Nair, former Chairman, JLL India and has worked in the Wealth Management Team at TATA Capital where he was awarded the National Award for Exemplary Performance. He is a perfect blend of Corporate Experience along with stellar education credentials of D.Litt., Ph.D., LL.M, LL.B, MBA and BMS from prestigious institutions like JBIMS, GLC, Narsee Monjee, ITM and Department of Law, University of Mumbai.

Dr. Harshul holds the World Record for "Maximum Degree from Single University" and his World Record is mentioned in World Book of Records London, The British World Records, International Book of Records, International Talent Book of Records, Exclusive World Record, Asian World Records, Global Records & Research Foundation, Amazing Indian Records, World Records India, India Book of Records, Kohinoor Vidyasamrat, Champion Book of World Record, High Range Book of World Records etc.

He also holds the World Record for "Maximum Books Authored & Published in a Year" for authoring and publishing 12 Real Estate Books in the year 2021 in English Language. Dr. Harshul is awarded as "Author of the Year" at the prestigious CNBC Awaaz Real Estate Excellence Awards 2022 held at Taj Lands End, Mumbai. He has also been awarded by ZEE Business as the Author of the Year in 2023 and by Realty Quarter in 2024 at the 7th Real Estate and Construction Industry Leadership Awards 2024. Dr. Harshul has been awarded as "Real Estate Author of the Year" multiple times.

Dr. Harshul was awarded Doctorate (Ph.D.) for his Thesis on REITs (Real Estate Investment Trusts) which is first such thesis in India on the said subject and the Thesis is also available in the form of a book. Apart from this he is an NSE Certified Market Professional - Level 4 and has done a course on 'Strategic Real Estate Management' from ISB, Hyderabad.

Dr. Harshul is "Chairman: Statistics & Standards" at CREDAI National, which has more than 13,300 Real Estate Developers as its Members and has presence in 230 Cities (21 State Chapters). He is Joint Secretary of CREDAI MCHI and heads its Statistics & Research Wing. CREDAI MCHI is a leading Real Estate Developers Association of MMR having 1,800 members across its 14 Units. Dr. Harshul is presently the "Chairman: C Suite Committee" at CREDAI National Youth Wing from 2024.

Dr. Harshul is also an Amazon Best Selling Author and has authored 25 books on the Real Estate Sector and General Management, making his books one of India's most comprehensive literatures on Real Estate Sector. Some of his books are: Real Estate Laws, Reality of Realty, Real Estate Valuation, Affordable Housing, NBFC & HFC Crisis, Fractional Ownership & REITs, Insolvency & Bankruptcy Code, Self-Redevelopment &

Reviving Stalled Projects, Digitalizing Real Estate Sector in Built Environment, Building Information Modeling, Green Buildings, Facility Management, COVID-O-NOMICS, Luxury Retail, Alternative Real Estate, Judicial Journey under RERA, Self-Redevelopment and Reviving Stalled Projects, NCLT & IBC in Real Estate Sector, ERA POST RERA, Funding Options for Developers, FSI – A Development Control Tool, The Redevelopment Guide, RERA Simplified, Real Estate Financing Options, Real Estate Dictionary, Homebuyers Handbook etc. He regularly writes articles for fortnightly business magazine "Property House" and may other newspapers and journals.

Dr. Harshul is Associate Professor at ITM University and is also a Ph.D. Guide/Supervisor with them. He was a Visiting Faculty and Guest Lecturer at the prestigious RICS School of Built Environment, Mumbai Campus. He taught the subject 'Real Estate Development Process' to Management Students at the Mumbai Campus. He was also a Guest Lecturer at REMI - The Real Estate Management Institute, Mumbai. He was Invited to conduct Session on REITs in India for Developers Members of NAREDCO and was one of the youngest Member Developer to do so. He has also delivered a lecture at PEATA (I) on Future of Realty. He is also a renowned moderator for panels discussing various aspects of Realty and has moderated more than 60 panel discussions so far.

Dr. Harshul has recently embarked his research journey for his second Ph.D. which he is pursuing from the Department of Law, University of Mumbai under the guidance of Former HOD of the Department. His thesis is on the topic of RERA and will be the first Ph.D. in Law thesis in India on RERA.

Dr. Harshul is also the Founding Member of the "RERA Practitioners' Welfare Association" and the Founding Member of "IRIYA Realty Intelligentsia and Advisory Foundation of India" which comprises of Innovation Centre, Think Tank and Centre of Excellence. Dr. Harshul is also part of the Managing Committee of IBG (India Business Group). Dr. Harshul is a Founding Member at the 500 MBA Club and also a Mentor at the Founder Institute which is the world's most proven network to turn ideas into fundable startups and startups into global businesses.

Disclaimer

Data Source and Limitations:

1. This data is derived from the MahaRERA website, where real estate projects data is publicly available.
2. It is possible that some of this data could be incorrect, which may skew the analysis. Thus, data provided in this book should not be relied on for micro-level accuracy, but rather can be used to study macro-level trends.
3. For analysis, we assume that every new MahaRERA project registration means that new inventory has been launched in the market.
4. This data may also include units that are provided under Permanent Alternative Accommodation Agreements, which are not available for free sale.

Additional Important Considerations:

5. The analyses and projections contained in this book are based on data available as of the publication date. Real estate markets are dynamic and subject to rapid changes due to economic, regulatory, or other external factors.
6. Market classifications, neighbourhood boundaries, and property categorizations used in this book are based on the authors' methodology and may differ from other industry definitions or official designations.
7. This book does not constitute investment, legal, or financial advice. Readers should consult with appropriate professionals before making any real estate investment decisions.
8. Historical trends presented in this book are not guarantees of future performance. All real estate investments involve risk and may result in losses.
9. While every effort has been made to ensure the accuracy of the information presented, the authors and publisher assume no responsibility for errors, omissions, or discrepancies in the data.
10. References to specific properties, developments, or areas are for analytical purposes only and should not be construed as endorsements or recommendations.
11. The statistical methods employed in this analysis have inherent limitations, and alternative methodologies might yield different results.
12. Readers are encouraged to verify all critical information through independent sources before acting on any information contained in this book.

The authors and publishers have made every effort to provide accurate, comprehensive market analysis, but this book should be considered one of many tools in making informed real estate decisions, not the sole basis for such decisions.

Introduction

Mumbai, India's financial powerhouse, drives the nation's real estate market with its unique blend of limited space and enormous demand. As the city continues to evolve, understanding its property landscape has never been more crucial for success.

Since 2020, nearly 4,000 projects in Mumbai City have been registered under MahaRERA, comprising of more than 340,000 units. With such a high volume of construction activity concentrated in a limited area, it has become crucial to understand supply-demand statistics at a detailed, micro-level to truly grasp the state of Mumbai's real estate market. Where is most of the new supply being added? What is the breakdown of carpet areas and unit configurations within this new supply? This book aims to answer these questions by providing granular insights into nearly every major location in Mumbai City, allowing readers to assess how new supply trends may impact the real estate market in each micro-market.

This book offers a powerful tool for everyone involved in Mumbai's real estate market. Developers can identify emerging opportunities, investors can discover promising micromarkets, homebuyers can make informed decisions, and policymakers can better understand housing trends to shape effective regulations.

Our analysis examines the top micromarkets (by pincode) across Mumbai City, using authentic data from the official MahaRERA website to reveal exactly what's happening in each area. These selected pincodes cover more than 95% of all the new launches in the city's real estate market. We track new housing projects, showing how apartment sizes and types are changing to meet buyer needs.

The pages ahead take you on a neighbourhood-by-neighbourhood journey through Mumbai's real estate scene, with easy-to-understand maps, charts, and insights. Whether you're planning to build, invest, buy, or simply understand this dynamic market, this book provides the clear, actionable information you need to make smart decisions in Mumbai's competitive property landscape.

Snapshot of 2025: New Real Estate Launches in Mumbai City

42,643 units

New Launches in Mumbai in 2025
(Down 40% Year on Year)

746 sqft.

Average size of a new unit
(Up by 24% since 2021)

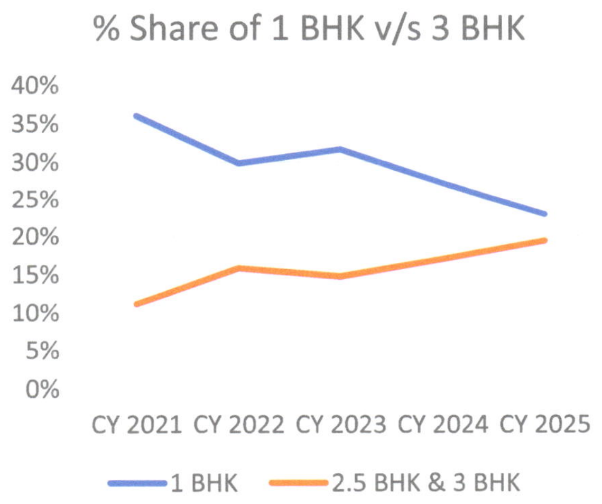

Share of 1 bedroom new launches have reduced by over 10% and share of 3 bedroom new launches have increased by 10% in the last 5 years.

Top 5 Micro-Markets by Supply Market Share (2025)

Rank	Micro-Market (Pin Code)	New Units (2025)	Market Share
1	Jogeshwari West/Oshiwara (400102)	2,395	6%
2	Malad West (400064)	1,968	5%
3	Mulund West (400080)	1,737	4%
4	Kandivali West (400067)	1,605	4%
5	Borivali West-Gorai (400092)	1,593	4%

Just these 5 neighborhoods account for nearly 22% of the entire city's new housing supply for 2025, highlighting a strong geographical concentration.

Analysis of New Real Estate Launches in Mumbai City (By Pincode)

Mumbai City

MUMBAI
CITY MAP
SANJAY GANDHI NATIONAL PARK
ARABIAN SEA
NAVI MUMBAI

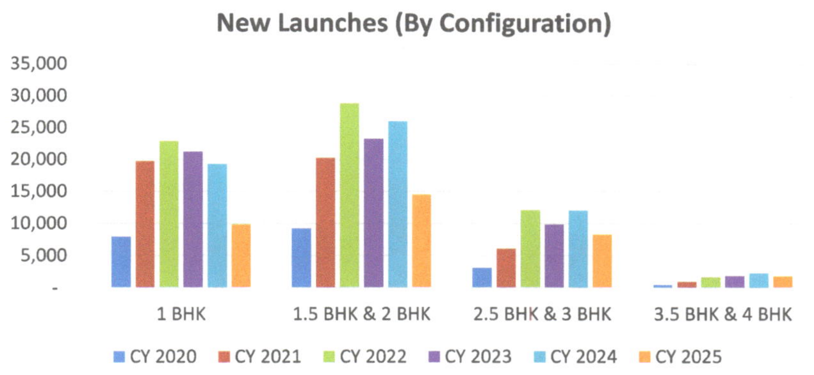

Mumbai City	CY2020	CY2021	CY2022	CY2023	CY2024	CY2025
Total Units	25,559	54,736	76,472	66,941	70,892	42,643
1 BHK	7,938	19,691	22,799	21,192	19,281	9,786
1.5 BHK & 2 BHK	9,231	20,237	28,793	23,251	26,021	14,485
2.5 BHK & 3 BHK	3,136	6,110	12,066	9,847	12,044	8,263
3.5 BHK & 4 BHK	491	1,000	1,678	1,878	2,320	1,826
Shops	722	2,106	2,632	2,541	2,926	2,597
Offices	2,652	2,555	5,439	4,753	4,816	3,059
Others	593	1,355	1,726	1,499	2,242	1,686

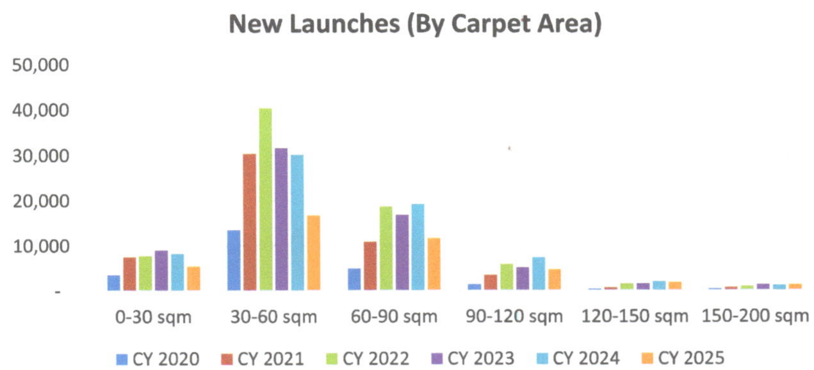

Carpet Area	CY2020	CY2021	CY2022	CY2023	CY2024	CY2025
0-30 sqm	3,495	7,538	7,675	9,026	8,294	5,372
30-60 sqm	13,467	30,374	40,279	31,614	30,161	16,675
60-90 sqm	4,953	10,793	18,590	16,786	19,185	11,606
90-120 sqm	1,428	3,439	5,820	5,178	7,366	4,637
120-150 sqm	377	599	1,478	1,556	2,003	1,818
150-200 sqm	430	668	965	1,306	1,158	1,238

400011 (Jacob Circle)

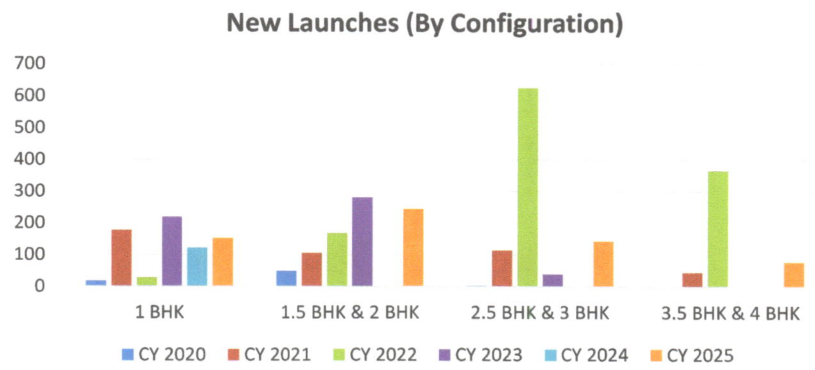

400011	CY 2020	CY 2021	CY 2022	CY 2023	CY 2024	CY 2025
Total Units	79	483	1200	568	172	763
1 BHK	17	177	28	219	122	152
1.5 BHK & 2 BHK	49	105	168	281	0	244
2.5 BHK & 3 BHK	3	114	624	39	0	143
3.5 BHK & 4 BHK	0	45	366	0	0	78
Shops	8	20	0	10	32	57
Offices	0	0	0	12	17	43
Others	2	22	2	7	1	34

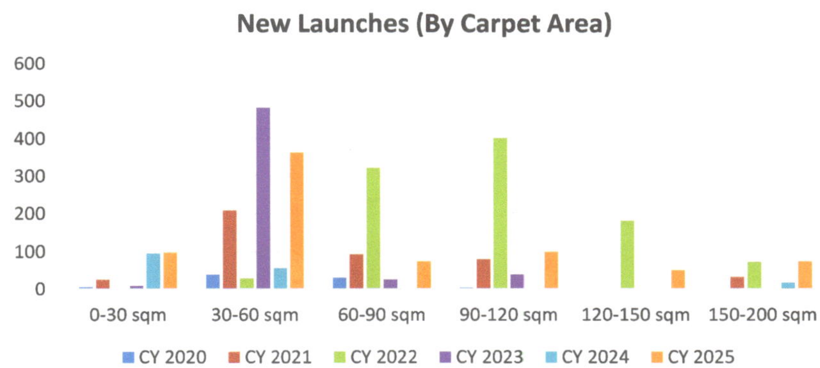

Carpet Area	CY 2020	CY 2021	CY 2022	CY 2023	CY 2024	CY 2025
0-30 sqm	5	25	0	9	96	97
30-60 sqm	39	208	28	482	56	363
60-90 sqm	31	93	321	25	0	74
90-120 sqm	4	80	401	39	0	99
120-150 sqm	0	1	180	1	2	51
150-200 sqm	0	32	72	0	17	74

400016 (Mahim/Matunga West)

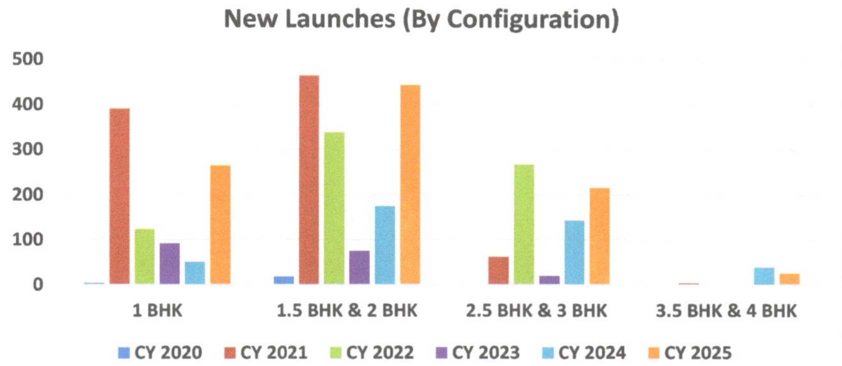

400016	CY 2020	CY 2021	CY 2022	CY 2023	CY 2024	CY 2025
Total Units	23	946	799	208	421	1229
1 BHK	4	391	123	92	51	264
1.5 BHK & 2 BHK	18	464	338	75	175	444
2.5 BHK & 3 BHK	1	62	266	20	143	216
3.5 BHK & 4 BHK	0	3	1	1	39	25
Shops	0	24	66	4	9	44
Offices	0	1	1	0	3	187
Others	0	0	1	12	1	46

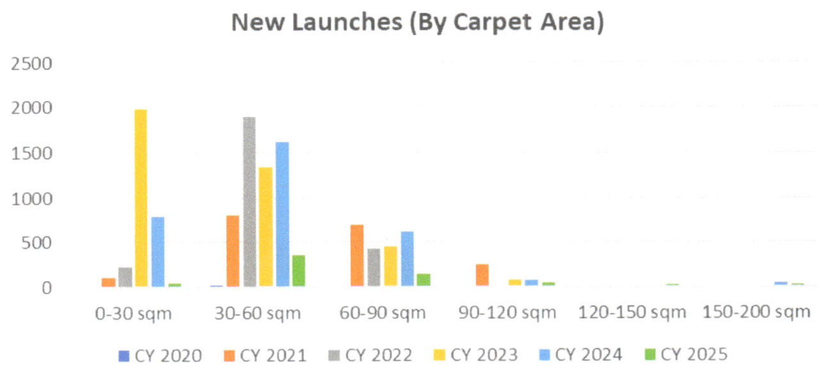

Carpet Area	CY 2020	CY 2021	CY 2022	CY 2023	CY 2024	CY 2025
0-30 sqm	0	11	47	12	30	43
30-60 sqm	6	628	174	145	80	350
60-90 sqm	15	112	322	31	134	566
90-120 sqm	1	33	255	17	109	204
120-150 sqm	1	16	0	2	65	35
150-200 sqm	0	2	0	1	3	7

400022 (Sion)

MUMBAI
CITY MAP
ARABIAN SEA
SANJAY GANDHI NATIONAL PARK
NAVI MUMBAI
401101
401105
401106
401107
401104
400610
400103
400068
400091
400066
400092
400607
400067
400101
400606
400608
400604
400601
400605
400602
400095
400064
400097
400080
400603
400063
400612
421204
400708
400081
400104
400065
400061
400102
400078
400053
400087
400060
400076
400042
400701
410208
400058
400069
400093
400096
400059
400083
400001
400710
400056
400057
400049
400099
400086
400709
400084
400054
400029
400075
400079
400703
400077
400055
400098
400070
400052
400089
400051
400024
400043
400705
400071
400022
400088
400050
400017
400074
400094
400706
400016
400037
400019
400085
400614
400028
400014
400025
400030
400031
400013
400015
400018
400012
400033
400011
400027
400034
400026
400010
400008
400007
400009
400004
400006
400002
400035
400021
400005

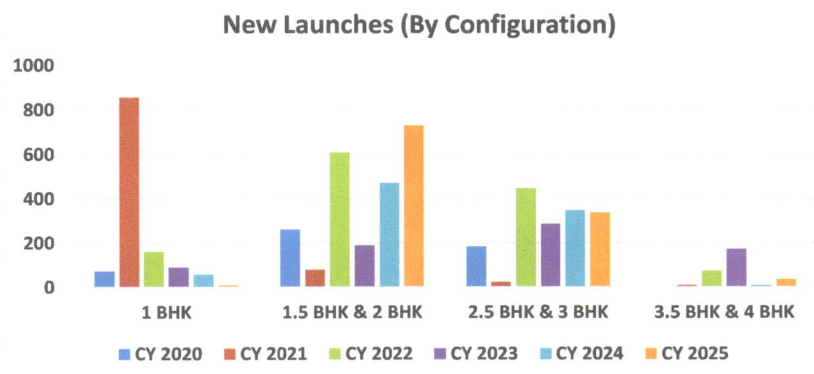

400022	CY 2020	CY 2021	CY 2022	CY 2023	CY 2024	CY 2025
Total Units	516	1053	1334	869	1211	1157
1 BHK	73	855	160	90	57	8
1.5 BHK & 2 BHK	260	78	607	188	471	729
2.5 BHK & 3 BHK	183	21	447	286	348	336
3.5 BHK & 4 BHK	0	8	72	172	8	34
Shops	0	18	26	14	47	31
Offices	0	3	4	80	219	2
Others	0	25	6	17	59	4

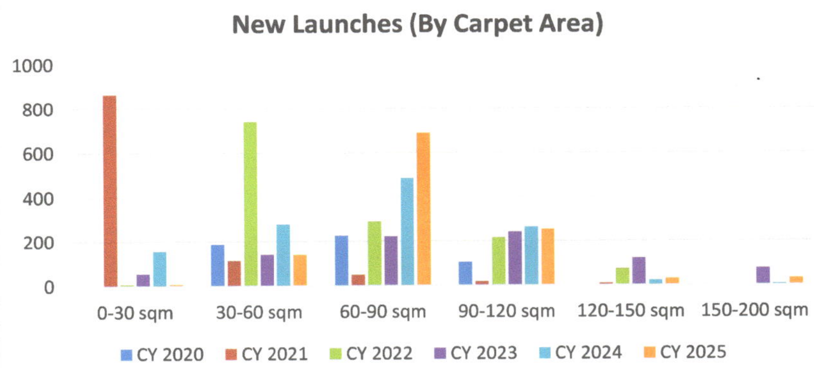

Carpet Area	CY 2020	CY 2021	CY 2022	CY 2023	CY 2024	CY 2025
0-30 sqm	0	864	8	54	155	8
30-60 sqm	186	113	738	140	277	139
60-90 sqm	226	48	289	222	485	688
90-120 sqm	104	17	214	242	263	253
120-150 sqm	0	9	72	120	22	28
150-200 sqm	0	1	2	74	5	29

400024 (Nehru Nagar/Kurla East)

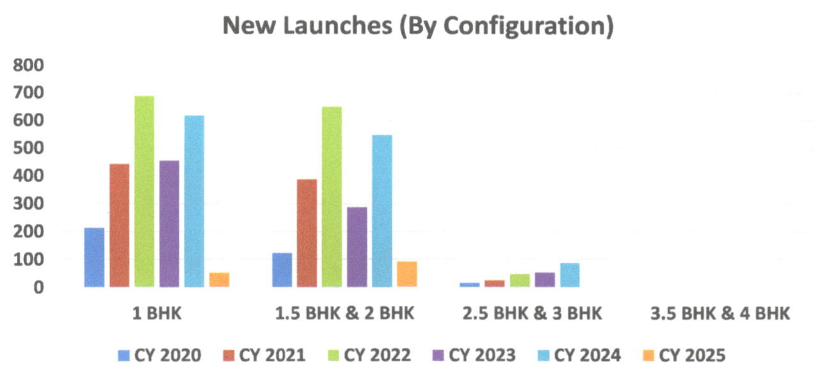

400024	CY 2020	CY 2021	CY 2022	CY 2023	CY 2024	CY 2025
Total Units	366	995	1426	832	1317	152
1 BHK	213	442	687	454	617	52
1.5 BHK & 2 BHK	123	387	649	287	547	92
2.5 BHK & 3 BHK	16	26	46	54	87	0
3.5 BHK & 4 BHK	0	0	0	0	0	0
Shops	12	15	7	12	56	7
Offices	2	5	0	17	2	0
Others	0	0	0	8	8	0

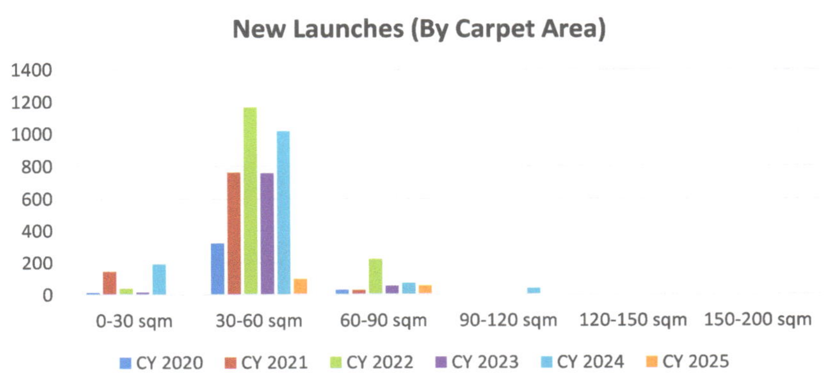

Carpet Area	CY 2020	CY 2021	CY 2022	CY 2023	CY 2024	CY 2025
0-30 sqm	13	144	37	17	192	3
30-60 sqm	322	761	1165	757	1016	96
60-90 sqm	30	29	220	54	70	52
90-120 sqm	1	0	3	2	37	0
120-150 sqm	0	1	0	1	0	0
150-200 sqm	0	0	0	1	1	0

400037 (Antop Hill)

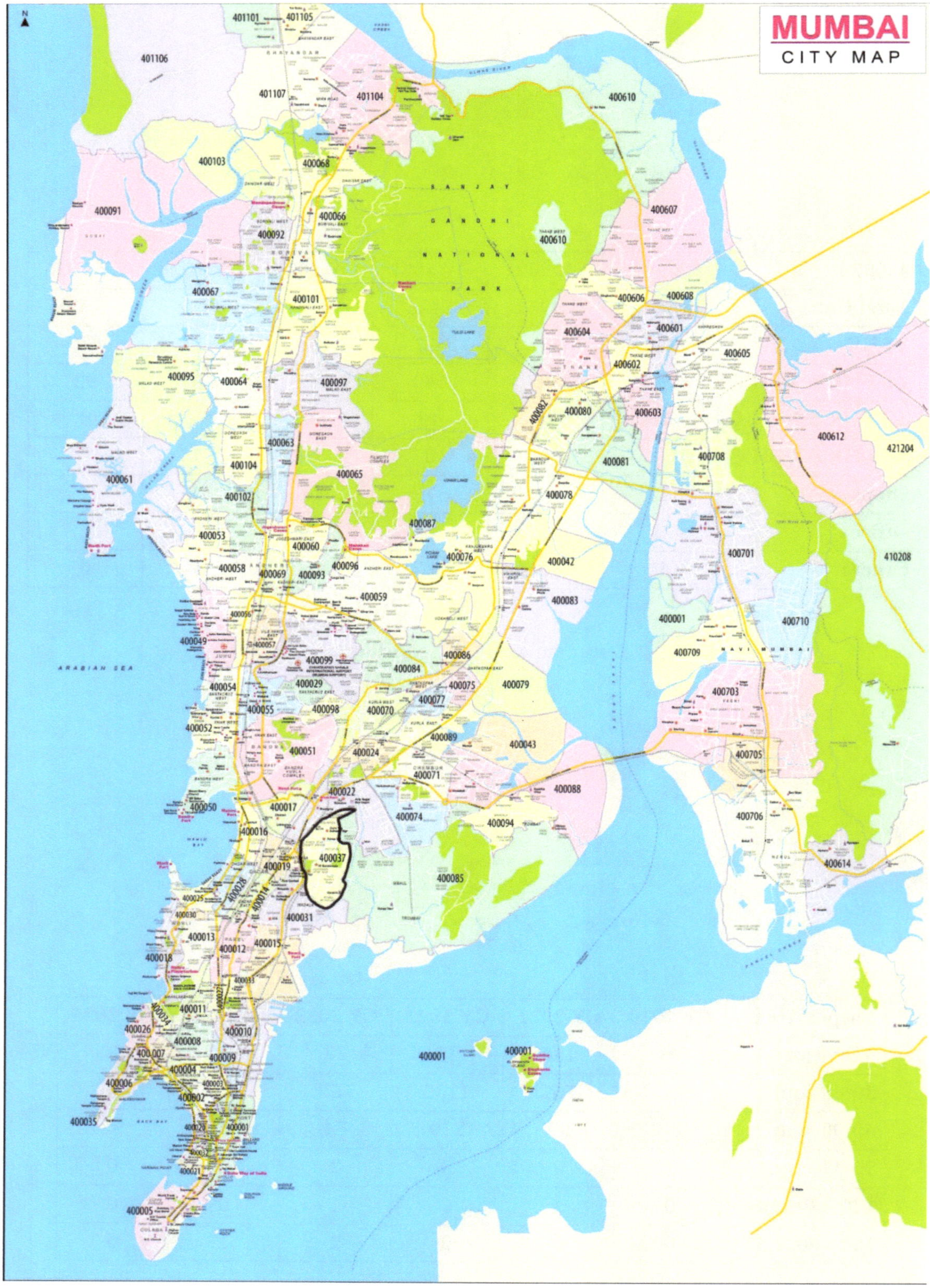

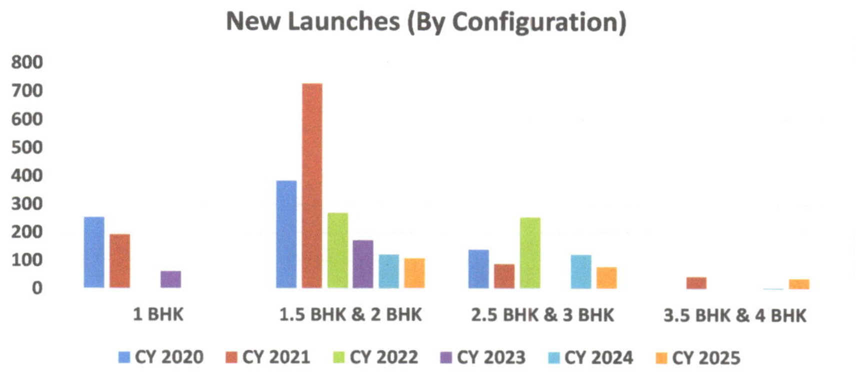

400037	CY 2020	CY 2021	CY 2022	CY 2023	CY 2024	CY 2025
Total Units	798	1052	543	242	248	239
1 BHK	254	192	0	61	0	0
1.5 BHK & 2 BHK	384	727	270	172	122	108
2.5 BHK & 3 BHK	140	88	254	0	122	78
3.5 BHK & 4 BHK	0	44	1	0	4	37
Shops	1	0	18	7	0	16
Offices	0	0	0	0	0	0
Others	0	0	0	2	0	0

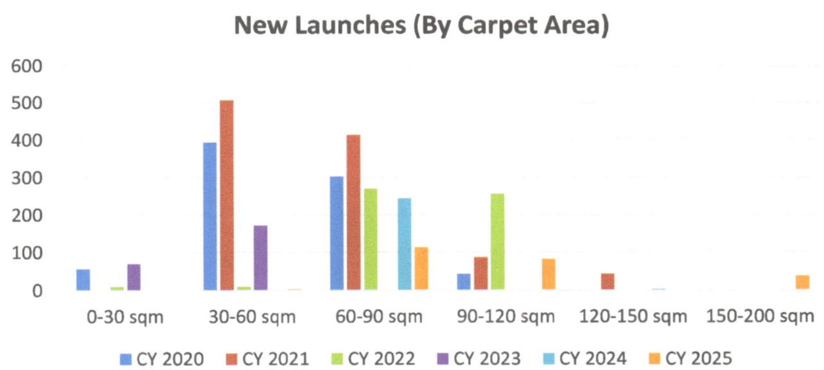

Carpet Area	CY 2020	CY 2021	CY 2022	CY 2023	CY 2024	CY 2025
0-30 sqm	57	1	9	70	0	0
30-60 sqm	394	506	9	172	0	3
60-90 sqm	303	414	269	0	244	113
90-120 sqm	44	87	256	0	0	82
120-150 sqm	0	44	0	0	4	2
150-200 sqm	0	0	0	0	0	38

400042 (Bhandup East)

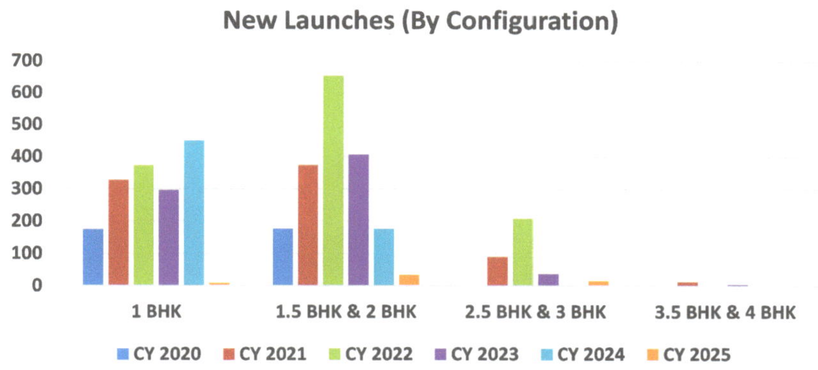

400042	CY 2020	CY 2021	CY 2022	CY 2023	CY 2024	CY 2025
Total Units	369	844	1567	857	643	57
1 BHK	175	327	372	296	450	8
1.5 BHK & 2 BHK	176	374	653	407	176	33
2.5 BHK & 3 BHK	0	89	207	37	0	15
3.5 BHK & 4 BHK	0	13	0	5	0	0
Shops	18	41	83	57	13	0
Offices	0	0	248	4	0	0
Others	0	0	0	31	0	0

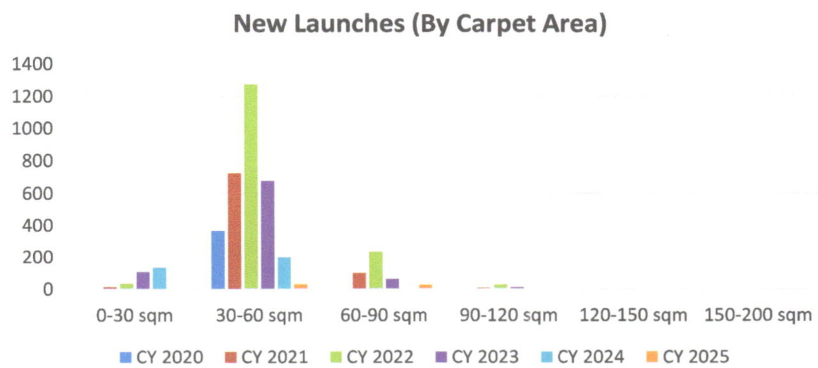

Carpet Area	CY 2020	CY 2021	CY 2022	CY 2023	CY 2024	CY 2025
0-30 sqm	0	14	33	107	135	1
30-60 sqm	366	724	1275	677	198	30
60-90 sqm	2	99	232	61	0	26
90-120 sqm	1	7	25	12	0	0
120-150 sqm	0	0	1	0	0	0
150-200 sqm	0	0	0	0	0	0

400050 (Bandra West)

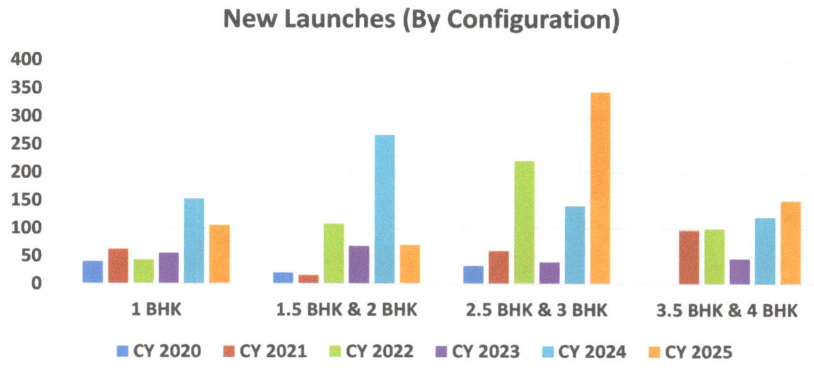

400050	CY 2020	CY 2021	CY 2022	CY 2023	CY 2024	CY 2025
Total Units	193	336	655	476	805	886
1 BHK	40	62	43	55	153	105
1.5 BHK & 2 BHK	20	16	108	68	267	70
2.5 BHK & 3 BHK	32	59	220	39	140	344
3.5 BHK & 4 BHK	0	97	99	46	121	150
Shops	0	70	16	10	27	56
Offices	80	0	125	210	2	76
Others	9	2	21	38	81	5

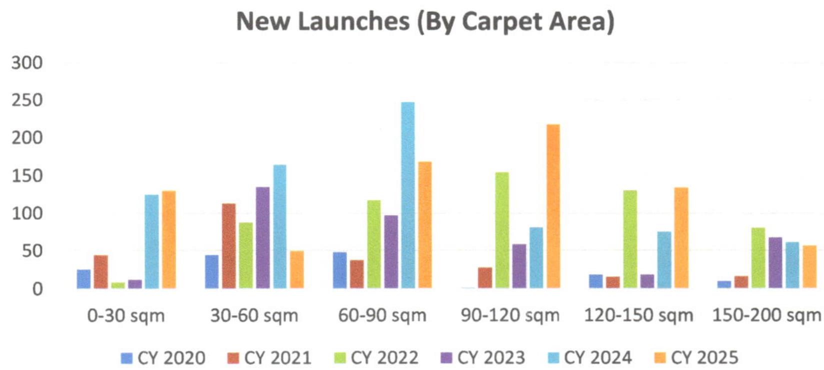

Carpet Area	CY 2020	CY 2021	CY 2022	CY 2023	CY 2024	CY 2025
0-30 sqm	25	44	8	12	125	130
30-60 sqm	44	113	87	135	164	49
60-90 sqm	48	37	117	97	247	168
90-120 sqm	1	27	154	58	81	217
120-150 sqm	18	15	130	18	75	134
150-200 sqm	10	16	80	67	61	56

400051 (Bandra East)

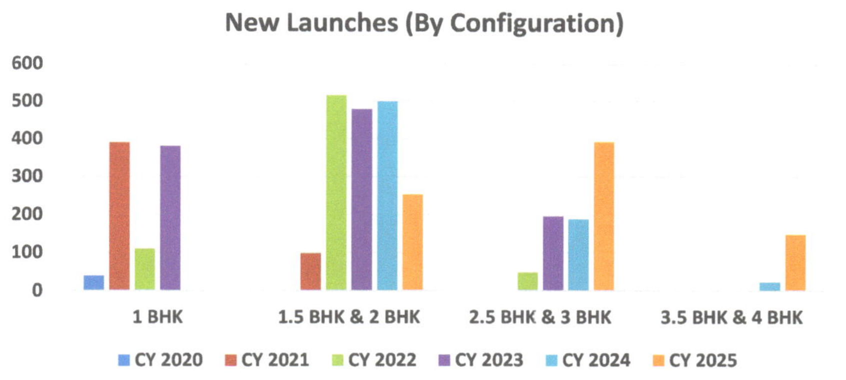

400051	CY 2020	CY 2021	CY 2022	CY 2023	CY 2024	CY 2025
Total Units	39	546	897	1349	722	1048
1 BHK	39	390	109	381	1	2
1.5 BHK & 2 BHK	0	98	516	480	500	252
2.5 BHK & 3 BHK	0	0	47	195	188	392
3.5 BHK & 4 BHK	0	0	0	0	23	148
Shops	0	3	69	72	10	5
Offices	0	0	1	221	0	245
Others	0	55	154	0	0	2

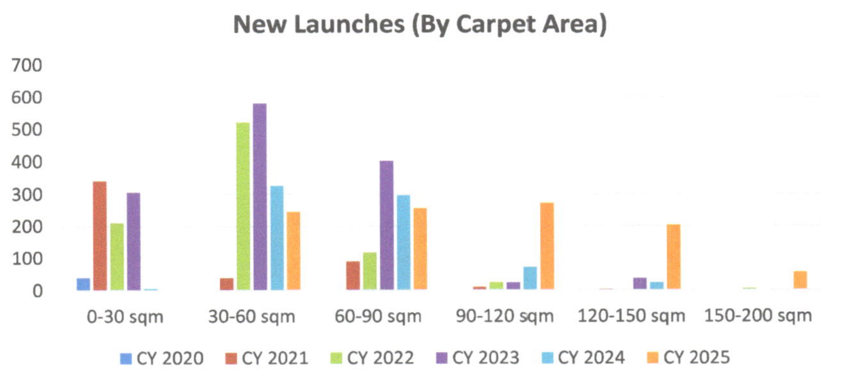

Carpet Area	CY 2020	CY 2021	CY 2022	CY 2023	CY 2024	CY 2025
0-30 sqm	39	341	209	306	6	0
30-60 sqm	0	38	520	580	326	244
60-90 sqm	0	89	116	401	296	255
90-120 sqm	0	10	24	23	71	272
120-150 sqm	0	3	0	37	23	203
150-200 sqm	0	1	5	0	0	55

400053 (Azad Nagar/Andheri West)

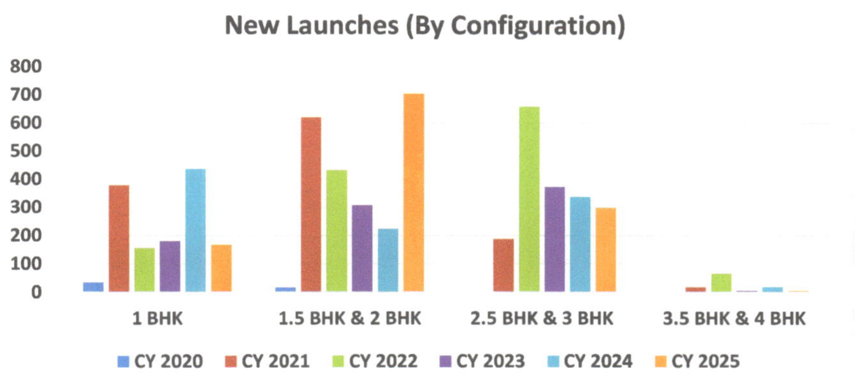

400053	CY 2020	CY 2021	CY 2022	CY 2023	CY 2024	CY 2025
Total Units	118	1437	1508	987	1092	1216
1 BHK	34	378	154	179	436	166
1.5 BHK & 2 BHK	16	620	432	307	224	703
2.5 BHK & 3 BHK	1	187	657	372	337	297
3.5 BHK & 4 BHK	0	18	65	5	19	4
Shops	0	41	28	52	21	33
Offices	0	191	165	4	0	9
Others	65	1	7	68	3	0

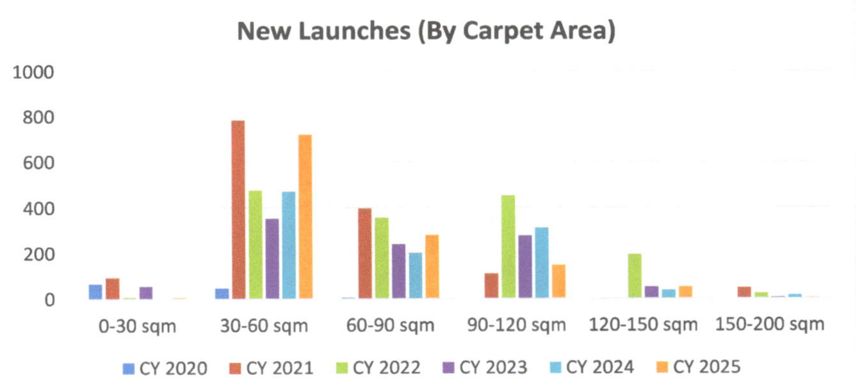

Carpet Area	CY 2020	CY 2021	CY 2022	CY 2023	CY 2024	CY 2025
0-30 sqm	66	93	7	55	0	5
30-60 sqm	47	783	474	352	471	719
60-90 sqm	5	396	356	240	201	279
90-120 sqm	0	109	451	276	311	146
120-150 sqm	0	1	193	52	36	50
150-200 sqm	0	47	22	5	15	4

400054 (Santacruz West)

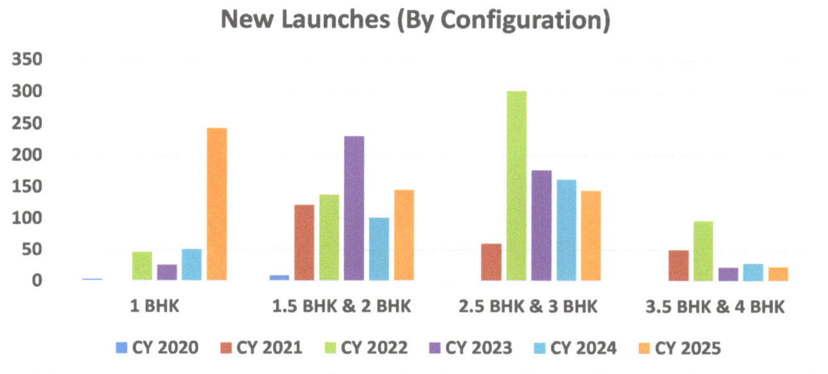

400054	CY 2020	CY 2021	CY 2022	CY 2023	CY 2024	CY 2025
Total Units	59	835	729	519	417	599
1 BHK	3	0	46	26	51	243
1.5 BHK & 2 BHK	9	121	137	230	101	145
2.5 BHK & 3 BHK	0	60	301	177	162	144
3.5 BHK & 4 BHK	0	50	96	22	29	23
Shops	0	1	23	13	30	13
Offices	1	38	99	27	4	14
Others	34	555	16	7	32	15

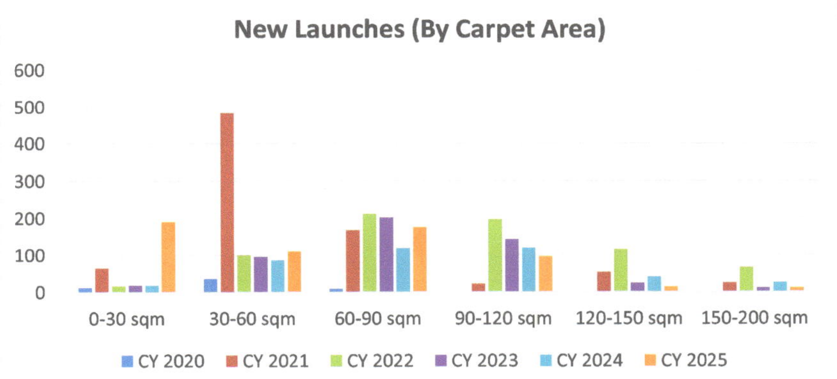

Carpet Area	CY 2020	CY 2021	CY 2022	CY 2023	CY 2024	CY 2025
0-30 sqm	12	64	16	18	18	190
30-60 sqm	36	484	99	96	86	110
60-90 sqm	9	167	211	202	118	175
90-120 sqm	2	22	196	142	119	96
120-150 sqm	0	53	114	23	40	13
150-200 sqm	0	24	65	11	25	10

400057 (Vile Parle East)

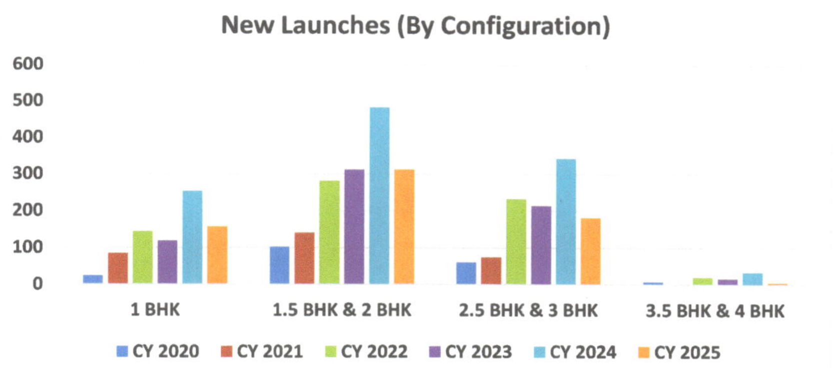

400057	CY 2020	CY 2021	CY 2022	CY 2023	CY 2024	CY 2025
Total Units	236	353	896	844	1357	730
1 BHK	24	84	143	118	253	157
1.5 BHK & 2 BHK	102	141	281	313	484	312
2.5 BHK & 3 BHK	61	74	231	214	343	181
3.5 BHK & 4 BHK	8	2	20	17	35	5
Shops	12	10	52	57	68	21
Offices	0	0	80	13	28	3
Others	28	42	48	98	92	13

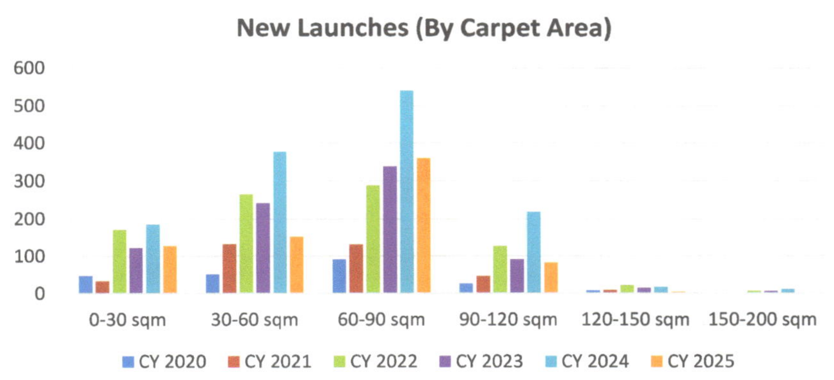

Carpet Area	CY 2020	CY 2021	CY 2022	CY 2023	CY 2024	CY 2025
0-30 sqm	47	33	170	122	185	127
30-60 sqm	51	132	265	242	377	152
60-90 sqm	91	131	288	338	540	360
90-120 sqm	26	46	126	91	219	82
120-150 sqm	8	9	21	15	17	3
150-200 sqm	0	2	6	6	11	2

400058 (Andheri West)

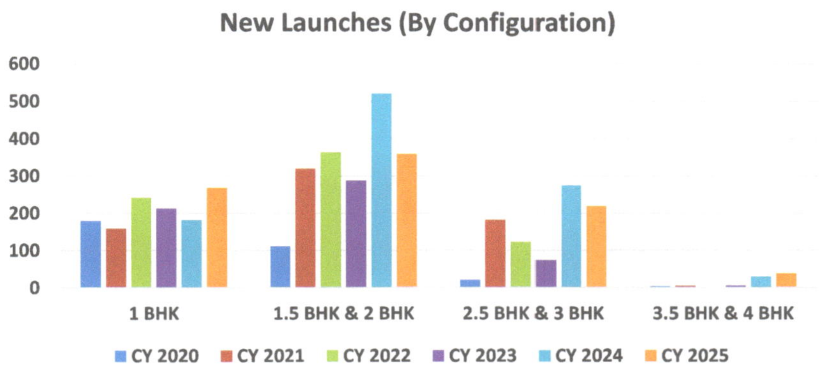

400058	CY 2020	CY 2021	CY 2022	CY 2023	CY 2024	CY 2025
Total Units	492	864	760	696	1160	976
1 BHK	179	159	241	213	182	268
1.5 BHK & 2 BHK	111	320	363	288	520	359
2.5 BHK & 3 BHK	21	182	122	74	275	219
3.5 BHK & 4 BHK	3	5	1	6	30	38
Shops	12	63	11	10	39	35
Offices	121	27	22	91	28	21
Others	1	10	0	7	17	32

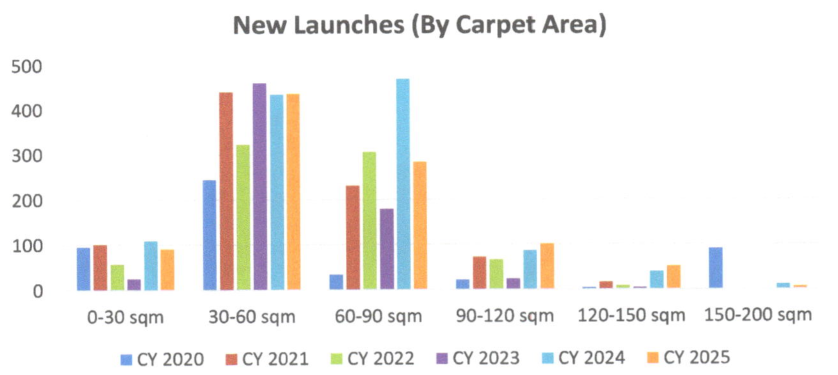

Carpet Area	CY 2020	CY 2021	CY 2022	CY 2023	CY 2024	CY 2025
0-30 sqm	96	101	57	25	109	91
30-60 sqm	244	441	322	461	435	437
60-90 sqm	34	231	305	180	470	283
90-120 sqm	22	72	66	24	86	101
120-150 sqm	5	16	8	5	39	51
150-200 sqm	91	1	0	0	12	6

400059 (Marol/Andheri East)

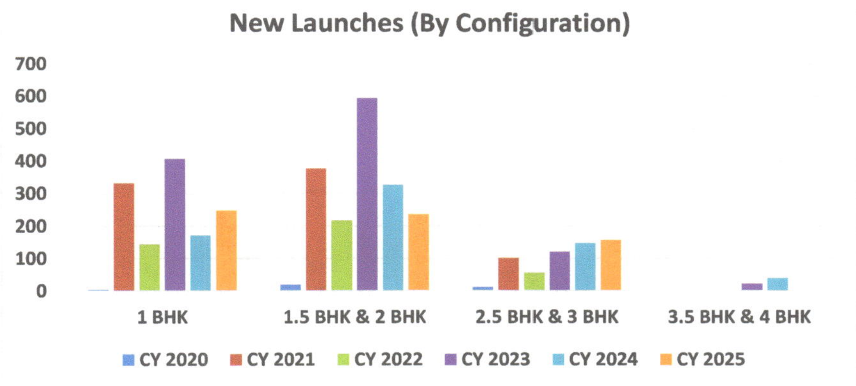

400059	CY 2020	CY 2021	CY 2022	CY 2023	CY 2024	CY 2025
Total Units	34	899	444	2014	1224	728
1 BHK	4	331	143	406	172	247
1.5 BHK & 2 BHK	19	376	217	593	326	236
2.5 BHK & 3 BHK	11	101	55	121	147	157
3.5 BHK & 4 BHK	0	0	0	22	40	0
Shops	0	70	10	18	20	15
Offices	0	20	3	145	518	52
Others	0	0	10	36	1	3

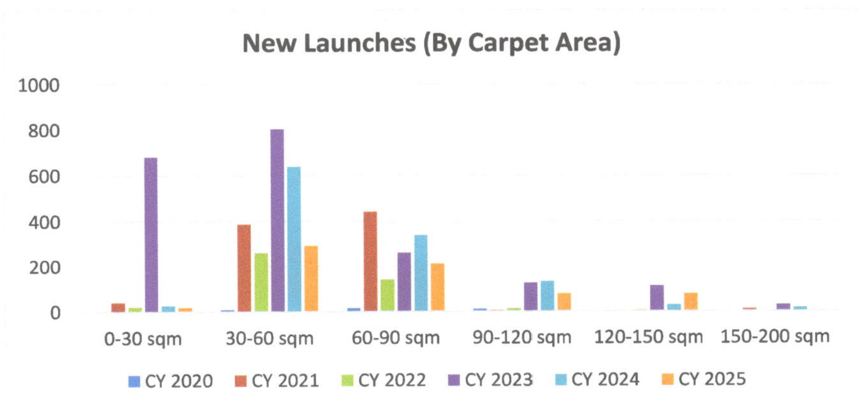

Carpet Area	CY 2020	CY 2021	CY 2022	CY 2023	CY 2024	CY 2025
0-30 sqm	0	40	19	681	26	18
30-60 sqm	8	387	258	803	638	291
60-90 sqm	15	442	139	260	338	211
90-120 sqm	11	4	11	124	131	75
120-150 sqm	0	2	4	110	27	76
150-200 sqm	0	10	1	28	15	2

400060 (Jogeshwari East)

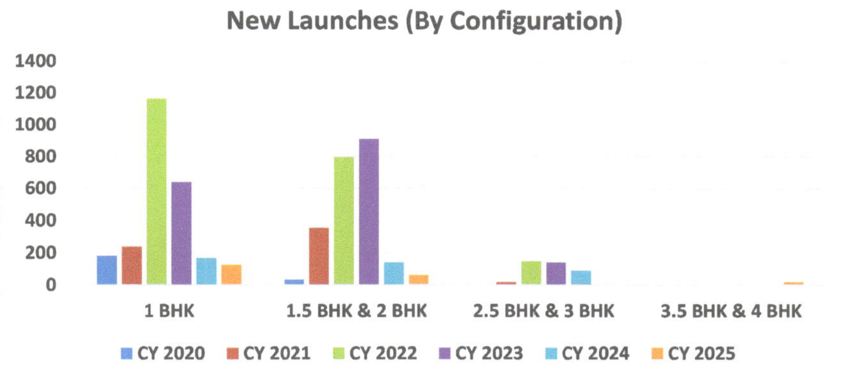

400060	CY 2020	CY 2021	CY 2022	CY 2023	CY 2024	CY 2025
Total Units	238	644	2478	2017	404	216
1 BHK	181	239	1162	638	168	126
1.5 BHK & 2 BHK	35	354	794	912	141	60
2.5 BHK & 3 BHK	0	18	147	141	90	0
3.5 BHK & 4 BHK	0	0	0	0	0	18
Shops	0	6	217	51	1	9
Offices	1	4	3	264	0	0
Others	2	22	14	1	4	3

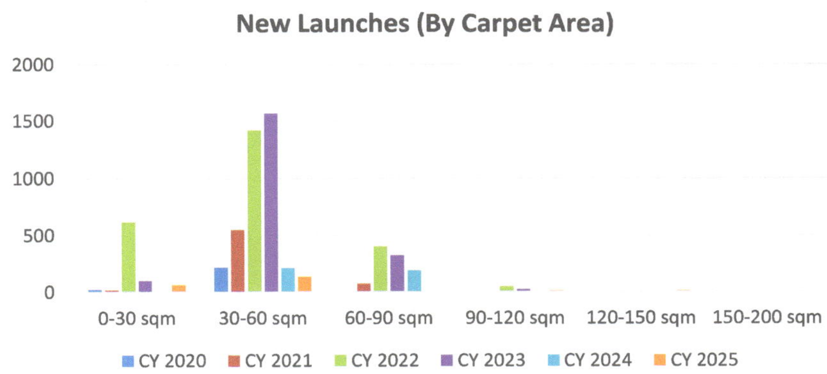

Carpet Area	CY 2020	CY 2021	CY 2022	CY 2023	CY 2024	CY 2025
0-30 sqm	21	17	615	100	3	62
30-60 sqm	217	549	1416	1567	209	132
60-90 sqm	0	71	400	322	186	4
90-120 sqm	0	1	45	23	2	9
120-150 sqm	0	6	1	5	1	9
150-200 sqm	0	0	0	0	3	0

400063 (Goregaon East)

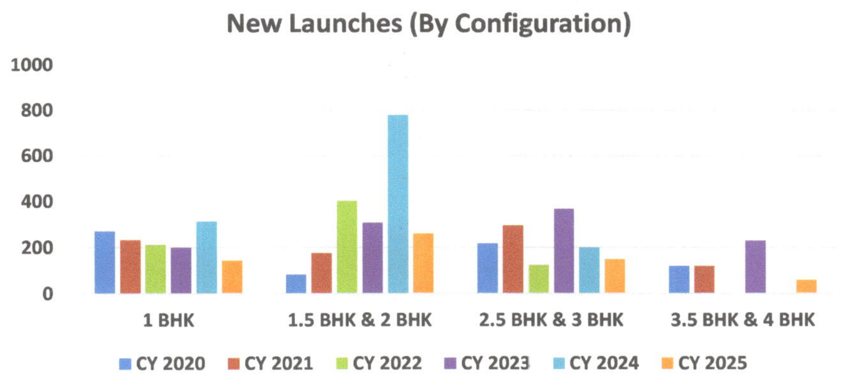

400063	CY 2020	CY 2021	CY 2022	CY 2023	CY 2024	CY 2025
Total Units	713	1224	1151	1256	1811	1152
1 BHK	271	232	211	200	313	142
1.5 BHK & 2 BHK	82	176	402	307	778	259
2.5 BHK & 3 BHK	217	295	122	367	200	148
3.5 BHK & 4 BHK	119	120	0	229	0	58
Shops	17	11	9	12	78	138
Offices	0	321	388	130	423	348
Others	3	0	5	3	18	15

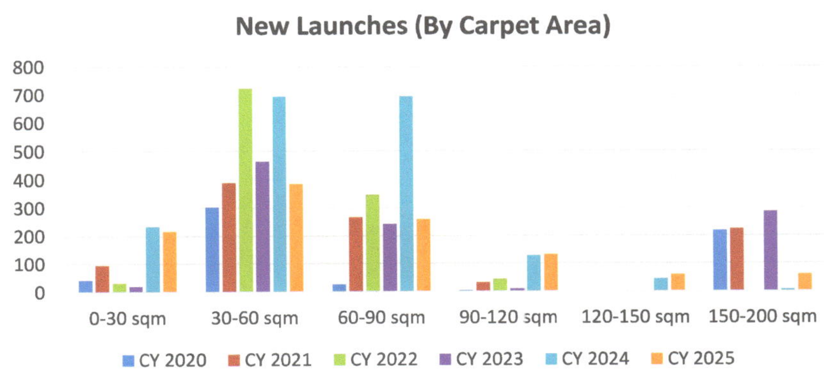

Carpet Area	CY 2020	CY 2021	CY 2022	CY 2023	CY 2024	CY 2025
0-30 sqm	43	94	32	21	234	216
30-60 sqm	302	389	722	463	694	385
60-90 sqm	27	266	346	242	694	259
90-120 sqm	4	33	44	10	128	131
120-150 sqm	1	0	2	3	45	59
150-200 sqm	217	223	2	285	7	59

400064 (Malad West)

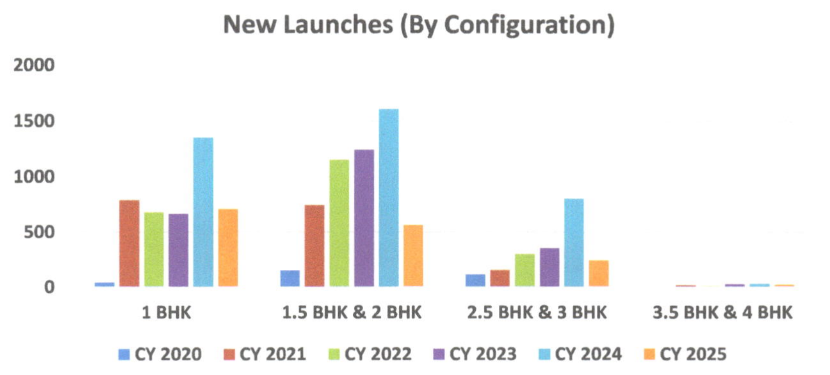

400064	CY 2020	CY 2021	CY 2022	CY 2023	CY 2024	CY 2025
Total Units	340	1927	2576	2692	4478	1968
1 BHK	41	788	676	666	1354	706
1.5 BHK & 2 BHK	150	744	1149	1244	1609	561
2.5 BHK & 3 BHK	116	155	297	354	801	239
3.5 BHK & 4 BHK	0	15	8	27	30	20
Shops	6	176	38	87	191	147
Offices	23	3	319	213	381	259
Others	3	13	86	87	87	9

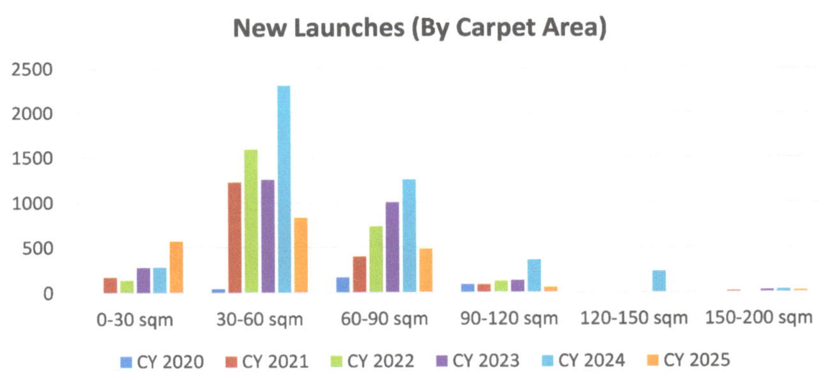

Carpet Area	CY 2020	CY 2021	CY 2022	CY 2023	CY 2024	CY 2025
0-30 sqm	2	171	134	279	281	569
30-60 sqm	45	1226	1586	1252	2311	830
60-90 sqm	166	396	730	1001	1256	478
90-120 sqm	90	86	120	132	356	55
120-150 sqm	1	3	3	0	229	6
150-200 sqm	0	17	2	28	36	20

400066 (Borivali East)

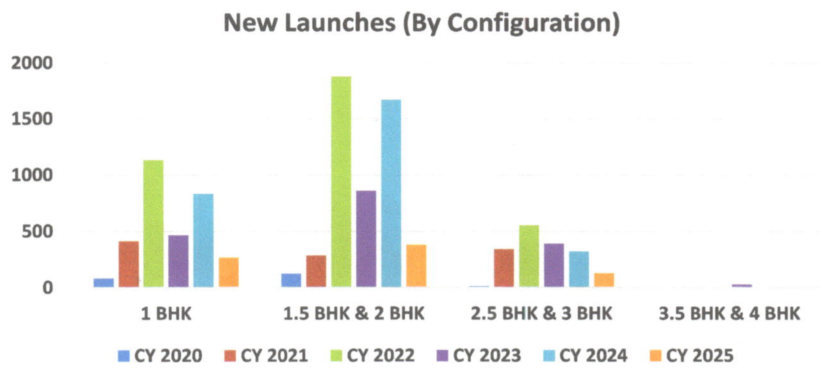

400066	CY 2020	CY 2021	CY 2022	CY 2023	CY 2024	CY 2025
Total Units	223	1224	4753	2284	3026	1066
1 BHK	82	414	1129	464	831	266
1.5 BHK & 2 BHK	122	284	1875	858	1673	379
2.5 BHK & 3 BHK	11	340	550	390	321	127
3.5 BHK & 4 BHK	0	0	6	28	2	0
Shops	3	35	113	111	136	106
Offices	0	25	830	352	8	164
Others	3	9	69	5	53	9

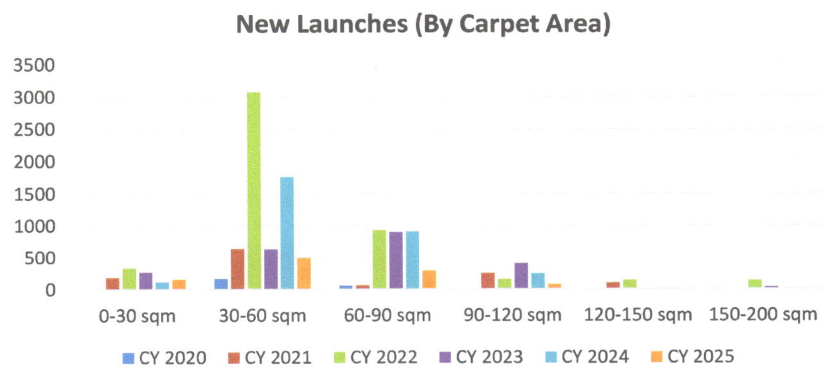

Carpet Area	CY 2020	CY 2021	CY 2022	CY 2023	CY 2024	CY 2025
0-30 sqm	3	185	328	265	113	154
30-60 sqm	162	632	3071	629	1757	486
60-90 sqm	55	60	925	897	907	286
90-120 sqm	3	245	145	400	239	70
120-150 sqm	0	94	135	5	5	4
150-200 sqm	0	0	130	31	2	11

400067 (Kandivali West)

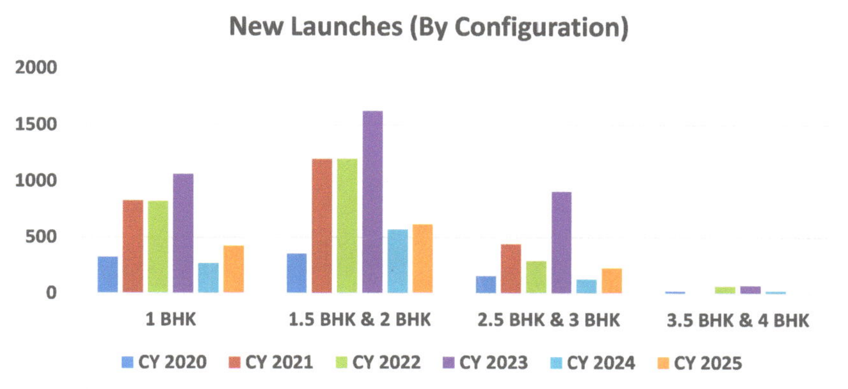

400067	CY 2020	CY 2021	CY 2022	CY 2023	CY 2024	CY 2025
Total Units	945	2778	2818	4300	1640	1605
1 BHK	321	824	818	1063	265	420
1.5 BHK & 2 BHK	351	1197	1197	1623	570	612
2.5 BHK & 3 BHK	154	437	286	909	126	225
3.5 BHK & 4 BHK	21	1	63	70	23	5
Shops	43	79	166	229	228	158
Offices	5	235	212	214	365	74
Others	23	4	68	155	50	110

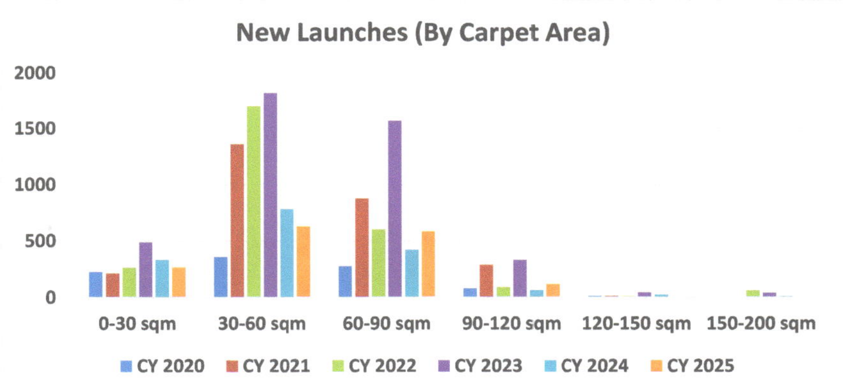

Carpet Area	CY 2020	CY 2021	CY 2022	CY 2023	CY 2024	CY 2025
0-30 sqm	222	209	259	489	331	262
30-60 sqm	357	1359	1698	1823	782	625
60-90 sqm	273	876	597	1568	422	582
90-120 sqm	79	284	87	330	62	116
120-150 sqm	12	13	8	42	23	6
150-200 sqm	1	1	58	39	9	6

400068 (Dahisar)

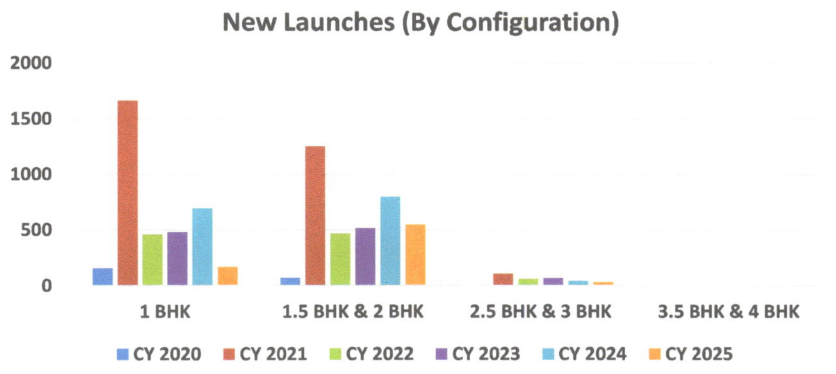

400068	CY 2020	CY 2021	CY 2022	CY 2023	CY 2024	CY 2025
Total Units	248	3121	1352	1107	1676	952
1 BHK	156	1662	457	480	692	167
1.5 BHK & 2 BHK	70	1252	465	516	799	547
2.5 BHK & 3 BHK	1	108	57	68	43	31
3.5 BHK & 4 BHK	0	0	0	0	0	0
Shops	0	52	150	21	70	71
Offices	0	19	215	0	67	122
Others	12	2	0	1	5	8

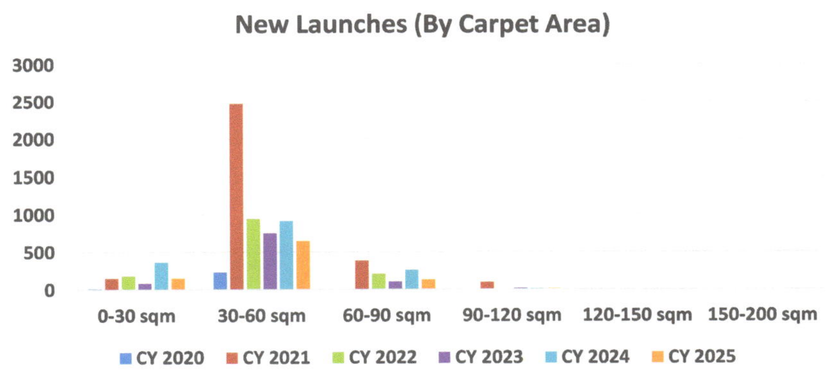

Carpet Area	CY 2020	CY 2021	CY 2022	CY 2023	CY 2024	CY 2025
0-30 sqm	15	154	179	87	367	152
30-60 sqm	232	2475	941	752	915	648
60-90 sqm	1	386	207	105	260	131
90-120 sqm	0	99	9	18	13	17
120-150 sqm	0	1	4	4	1	2
150-200 sqm	0	2	11	0	1	0

400069 (Andheri East)

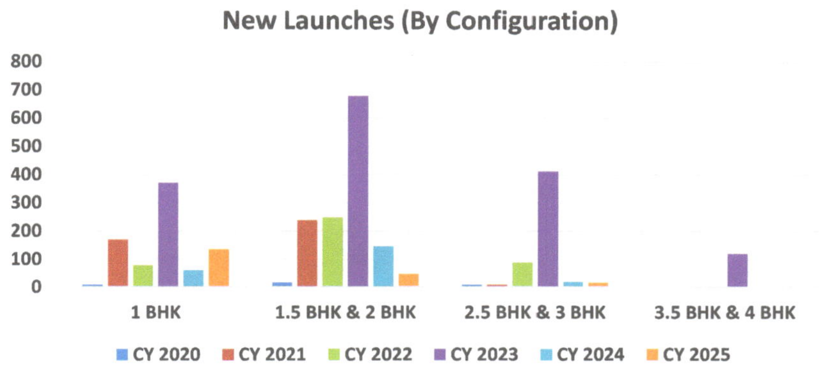

400069	CY 2020	CY 2021	CY 2022	CY 2023	CY 2024	CY 2025
Total Units	41	616	438	1812	254	328
1 BHK	8	170	77	370	61	135
1.5 BHK & 2 BHK	16	238	248	678	146	46
2.5 BHK & 3 BHK	8	9	87	412	18	15
3.5 BHK & 4 BHK	0	0	0	120	0	0
Shops	9	9	19	95	15	8
Offices	0	31	3	50	10	81
Others	0	0	1	58	1	43

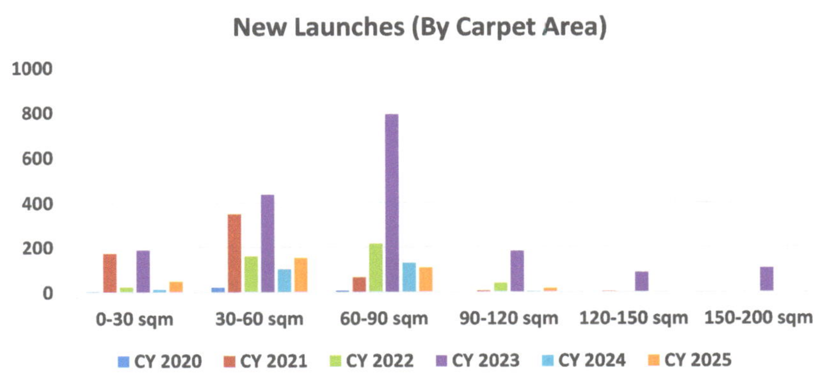

Carpet Area	CY 2020	CY 2021	CY 2022	CY 2023	CY 2024	CY 2025
0-30 sqm	4	172	23	188	14	48
30-60 sqm	24	351	158	438	103	152
60-90 sqm	10	67	215	792	130	108
90-120 sqm	3	8	40	183	5	17
120-150 sqm	0	4	2	87	1	2
150-200 sqm	0	0	0	106	0	1

400071 (Chembur)

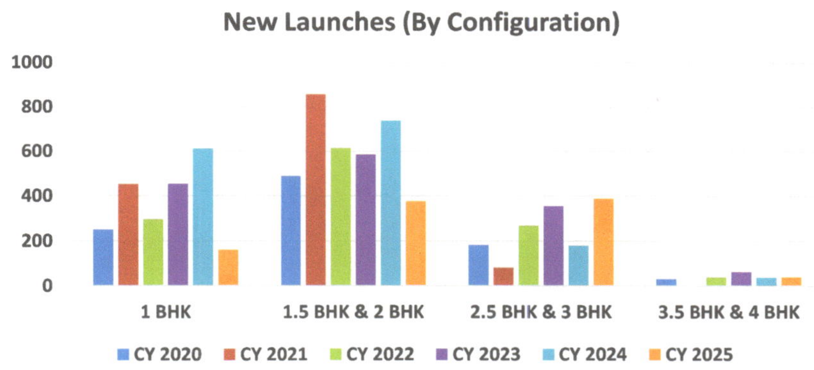

400071	CY 2020	CY 2021	CY 2022	CY 2023	CY 2024	CY 2025
Total Units	1039	1459	1344	2096	1758	1088
1 BHK	251	452	296	453	611	160
1.5 BHK & 2 BHK	488	857	613	586	738	376
2.5 BHK & 3 BHK	183	80	267	356	180	389
3.5 BHK & 4 BHK	31	1	38	63	38	40
Shops	0	48	64	125	59	51
Offices	29	20	60	7	95	40
Others	45	0	5	58	17	30

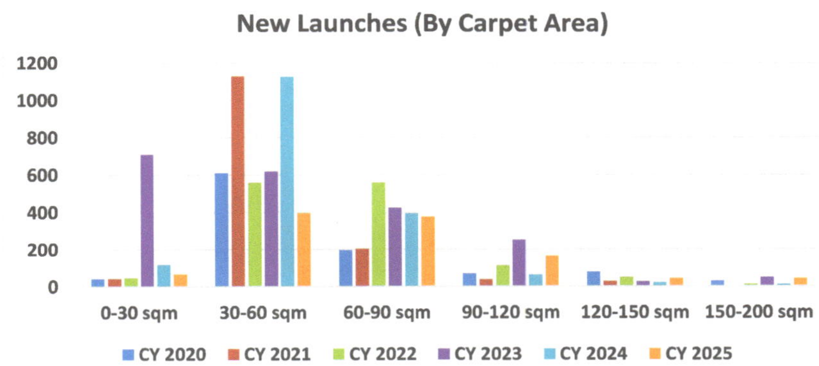

Carpet Area	CY 2020	CY 2021	CY 2022	CY 2023	CY 2024	CY 2025
0-30 sqm	43	43	46	709	118	66
30-60 sqm	610	1129	558	618	1127	396
60-90 sqm	198	204	557	424	395	377
90-120 sqm	69	38	110	250	62	163
120-150 sqm	77	27	48	26	21	43
150-200 sqm	29	2	11	48	10	40

400072 (Sakinaka/Chandivali)

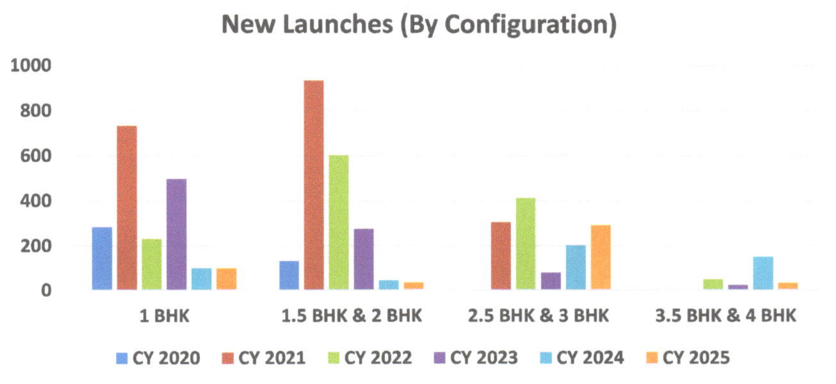

400072	CY 2020	CY 2021	CY 2022	CY 2023	CY 2024	CY 2025
Total Units	539	2118	1438	892	643	917
1 BHK	284	733	230	497	100	98
1.5 BHK & 2 BHK	131	934	601	275	44	33
2.5 BHK & 3 BHK	0	305	410	78	202	291
3.5 BHK & 4 BHK	0	0	48	23	150	31
Shops	120	108	27	19	44	103
Offices	0	0	121	0	0	157
Others	4	0	0	0	0	7

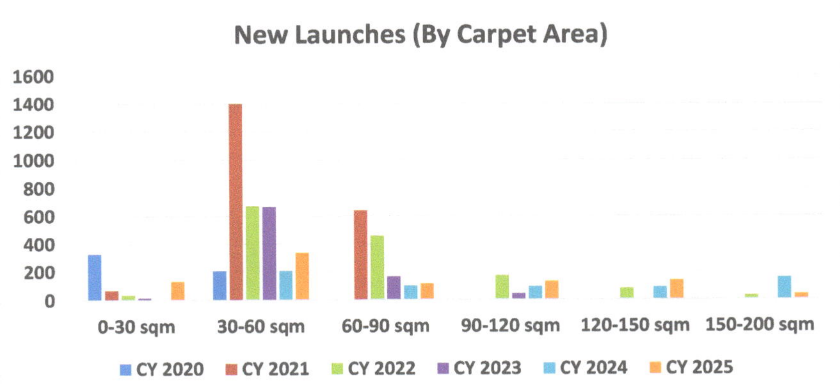

Carpet Area	CY 2020	CY 2021	CY 2022	CY 2023	CY 2024	CY 2025
0-30 sqm	327	69	35	18	3	130
30-60 sqm	205	1399	670	666	206	335
60-90 sqm	2	639	456	164	99	111
90-120 sqm	0	5	168	43	92	127
120-150 sqm	0	3	78	1	88	134
150-200 sqm	1	0	28	0	155	38

400074 (Mahul)

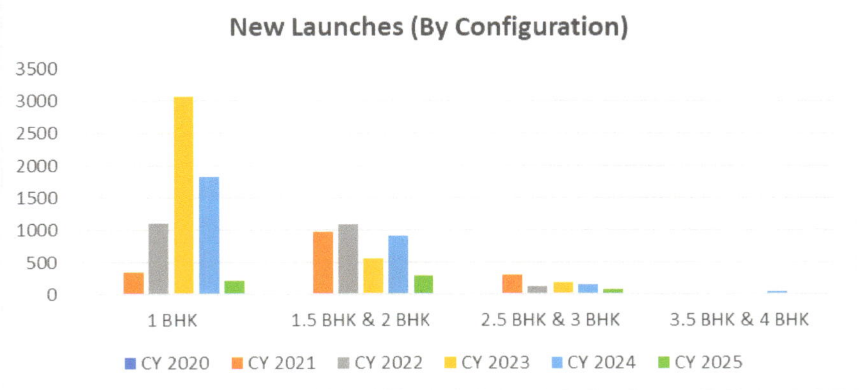

400074	CY 2020	CY 2021	CY 2022	CY 2023	CY 2024	CY 2025
Total Units	101	387	73	314	2175	248
1 BHK	52	171	50	28	1090	1
1.5 BHK & 2 BHK	44	76	22	133	691	239
2.5 BHK & 3 BHK	1	19	1	130	353	0
3.5 BHK & 4 BHK	0	0	0	0	1	0
Shops	0	5	0	23	39	8
Offices	0	0	0	0	0	0
Others	4	114	0	0	0	0

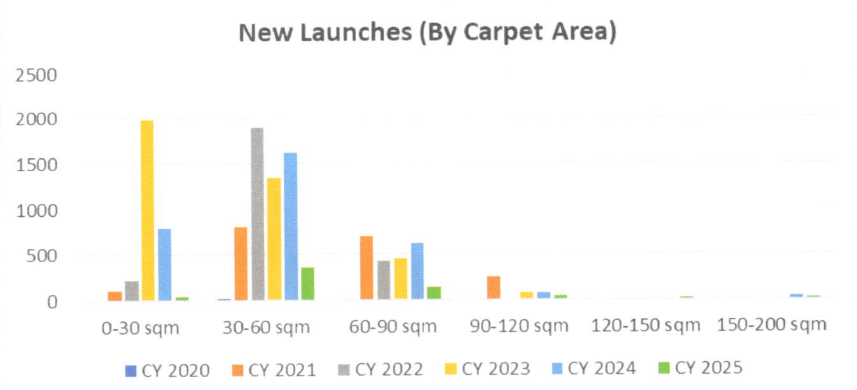

Carpet Area	CY 2020	CY 2021	CY 2022	CY 2023	CY 2024	CY 2025
0-30 sqm	4	24	0	16	73	0
30-60 sqm	80	198	65	28	1626	2
60-90 sqm	17	45	8	134	426	240
90-120 sqm	0	16	0	134	26	2
120-150 sqm	0	0	0	1	7	1
150-200 sqm	0	2	0	0	6	3

400075 (Ghatkopar East)

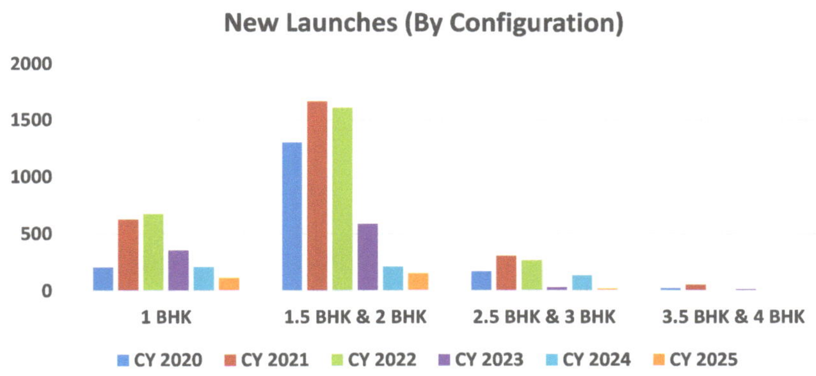

400075	CY 2020	CY 2021	CY 2022	CY 2023	CY 2024	CY 2025
Total Units	2002	2696	2792	1124	634	385
1 BHK	206	623	672	355	207	114
1.5 BHK & 2 BHK	1301	1663	1606	586	213	149
2.5 BHK & 3 BHK	171	306	264	31	136	15
3.5 BHK & 4 BHK	21	51	0	14	6	0
Shops	51	45	16	22	21	34
Offices	248	0	179	68	4	73
Others	4	6	6	46	0	0

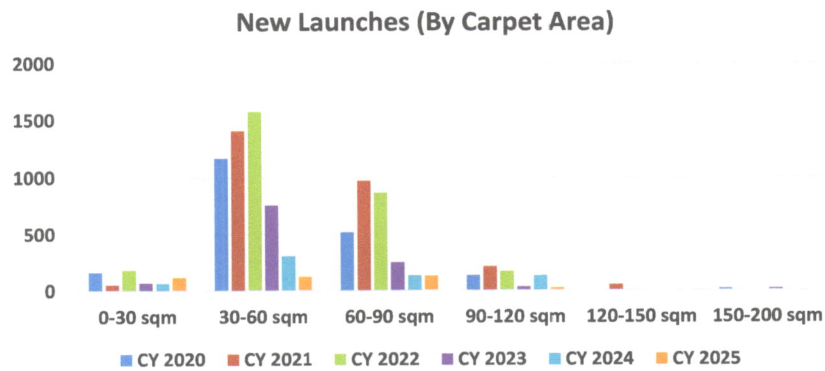

Carpet Area	CY 2020	CY 2021	CY 2022	CY 2023	CY 2024	CY 2025
0-30 sqm	163	51	178	69	66	116
30-60 sqm	1166	1407	1572	757	306	121
60-90 sqm	517	972	864	248	130	126
90-120 sqm	132	208	164	33	129	22
120-150 sqm	2	49	0	0	2	0
150-200 sqm	16	5	0	17	1	0

400077 (Ghatkopar East)

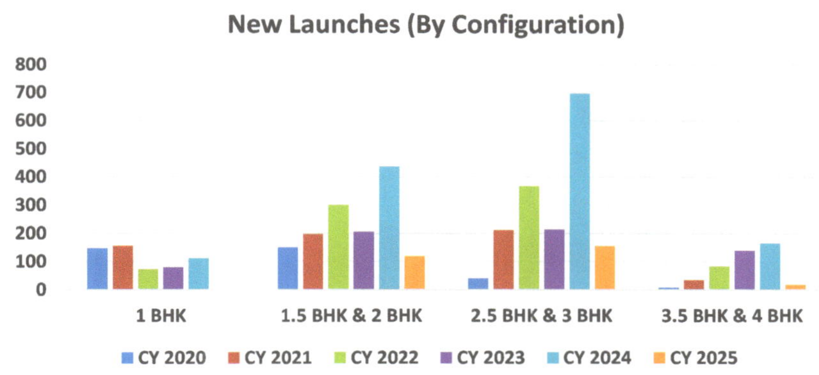

400077	CY 2020	CY 2021	CY 2022	CY 2023	CY 2024	CY 2025
Total Units	490	965	882	973	1897	613
1 BHK	147	156	72	79	111	3
1.5 BHK & 2 BHK	151	197	300	206	437	118
2.5 BHK & 3 BHK	40	212	366	213	696	155
3.5 BHK & 4 BHK	9	35	83	140	166	18
Shops	0	47	15	54	82	59
Offices	136	246	1	146	156	256
Others	3	69	34	116	164	2

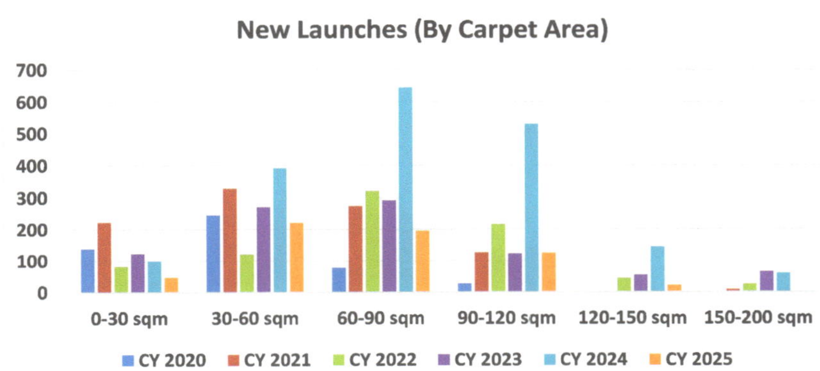

Carpet Area	CY 2020	CY 2021	CY 2022	CY 2023	CY 2024	CY 2025
0-30 sqm	139	223	82	123	99	46
30-60 sqm	246	329	120	271	392	221
60-90 sqm	78	274	320	292	645	194
90-120 sqm	26	126	215	122	529	124
120-150 sqm	1	0	42	53	144	21
150-200 sqm	0	8	24	64	59	2

400078 (Bhandup West)

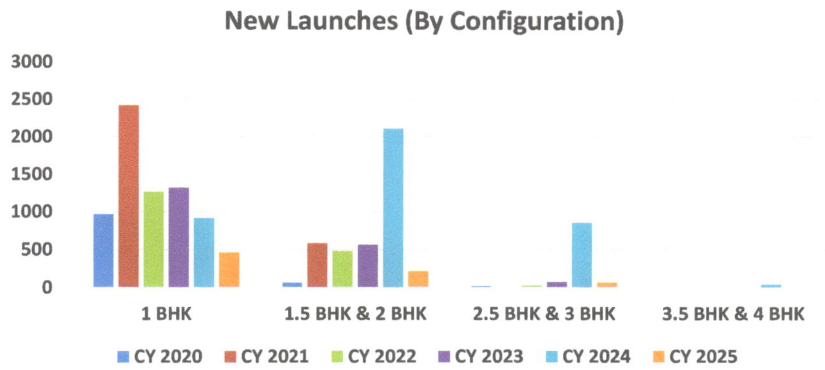

400078	CY 2020	CY 2021	CY 2022	CY 2023	CY 2024	CY 2025
Total Units	1616	3581	1986	2339	4227	954
1 BHK	966	2418	1262	1321	917	462
1.5 BHK & 2 BHK	68	585	480	566	2110	214
2.5 BHK & 3 BHK	18	9	22	75	855	67
3.5 BHK & 4 BHK	0	0	0	1	46	0
Shops	52	76	49	111	147	66
Offices	129	41	37	107	158	1
Others	21	85	45	25	38	77

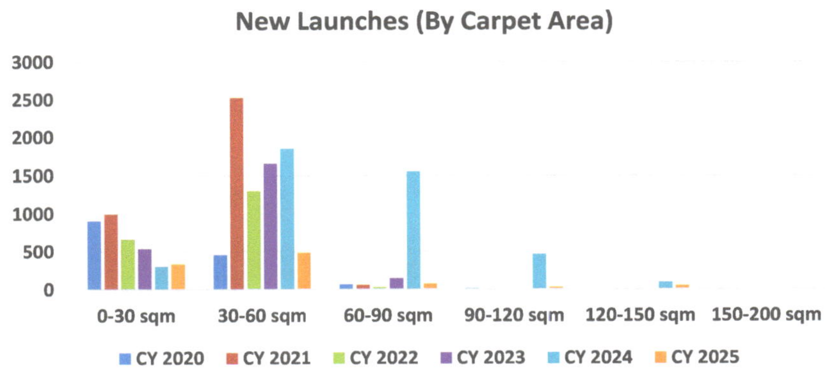

Carpet Area	CY 2020	CY 2021	CY 2022	CY 2023	CY 2024	CY 2025
0-30 sqm	907	994	658	535	303	330
30-60 sqm	454	2525	1298	1653	1849	480
60-90 sqm	67	57	22	146	1551	72
90-120 sqm	13	5	2	3	456	25
120-150 sqm	1	0	3	0	91	44
150-200 sqm	3	0	0	0	8	0

400080 (Mulund West)

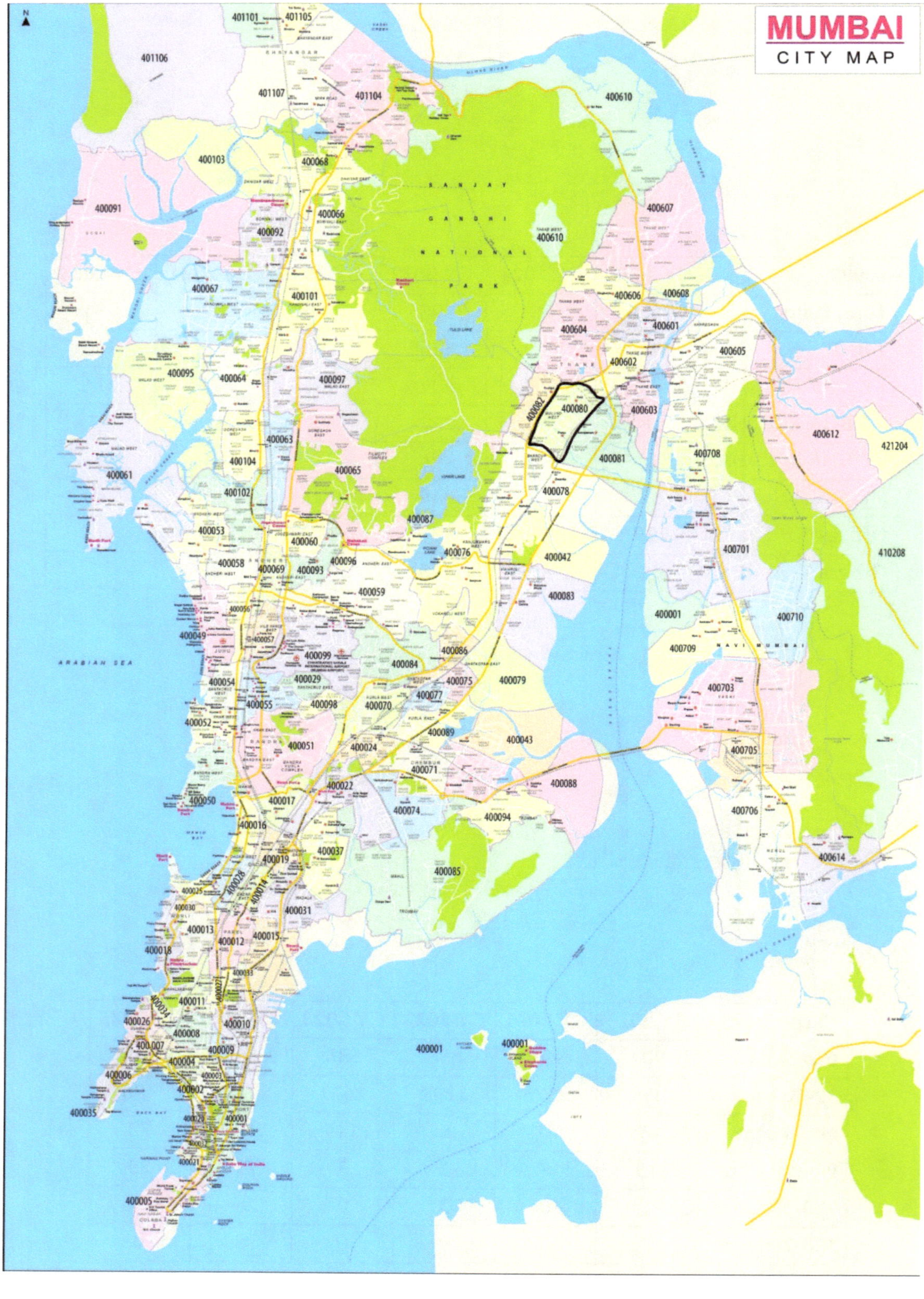

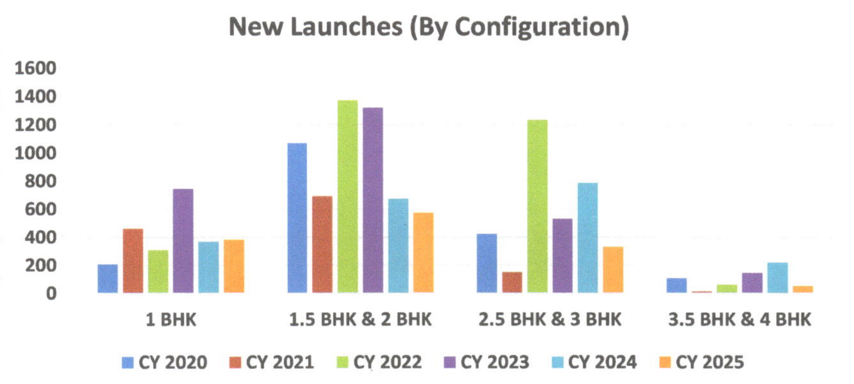

400080	CY 2020	CY 2021	CY 2022	CY 2023	CY 2024	CY 2025
Total Units	1883	1380	3754	3719	2478	1737
1 BHK	208	459	305	743	366	380
1.5 BHK & 2 BHK	1069	692	1372	1321	673	572
2.5 BHK & 3 BHK	423	150	1231	531	787	330
3.5 BHK & 4 BHK	108	14	60	145	221	52
Shops	6	21	75	112	131	119
Offices	0	6	471	721	50	127
Others	48	1	130	117	179	120

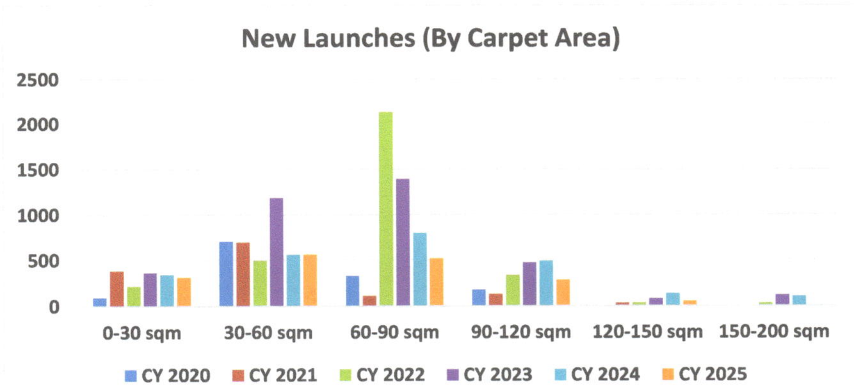

Carpet Area	CY 2020	CY 2021	CY 2022	CY 2023	CY 2024	CY 2025
0-30 sqm	93	384	213	362	340	310
30-60 sqm	704	695	492	1187	561	562
60-90 sqm	327	111	2129	1393	797	517
90-120 sqm	174	130	329	472	487	278
120-150 sqm	4	32	33	81	133	52
150-200 sqm	1	0	26	118	105	7

400081 (Mulund East)

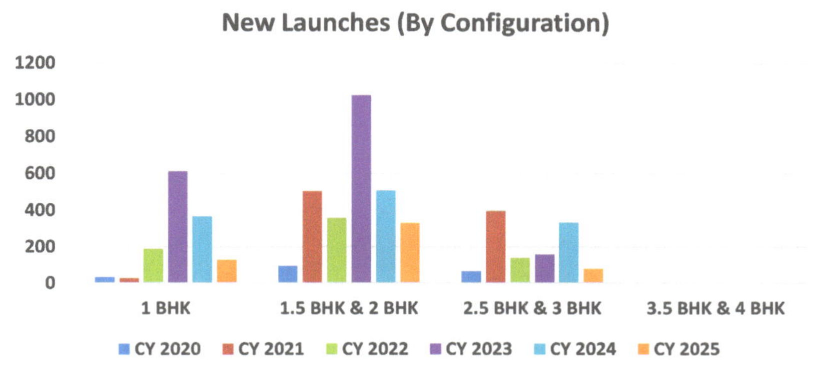

400081	CY 2020	CY 2021	CY 2022	CY 2023	CY 2024	CY 2025
Total Units	220	988	719	1930	1296	688
1 BHK	33	26	186	612	366	126
1.5 BHK & 2 BHK	94	504	356	1025	508	329
2.5 BHK & 3 BHK	65	394	136	157	333	77
3.5 BHK & 4 BHK	0	3	1	0	3	0
Shops	2	28	27	32	41	53
Offices	3	8	0	1	5	40
Others	10	1	1	89	38	44

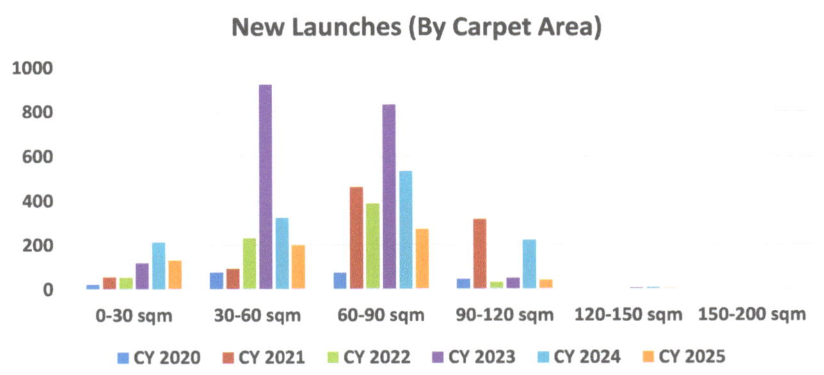

Carpet Area	CY 2020	CY 2021	CY 2022	CY 2023	CY 2024	CY 2025
0-30 sqm	23	55	51	119	213	130
30-60 sqm	75	92	228	925	322	198
60-90 sqm	74	461	385	832	533	269
90-120 sqm	45	316	29	49	222	40
120-150 sqm	0	2	1	5	6	3
150-200 sqm	2	0	0	0	0	0

400083 (Kannamwar Nagar/Tagore Nagar)

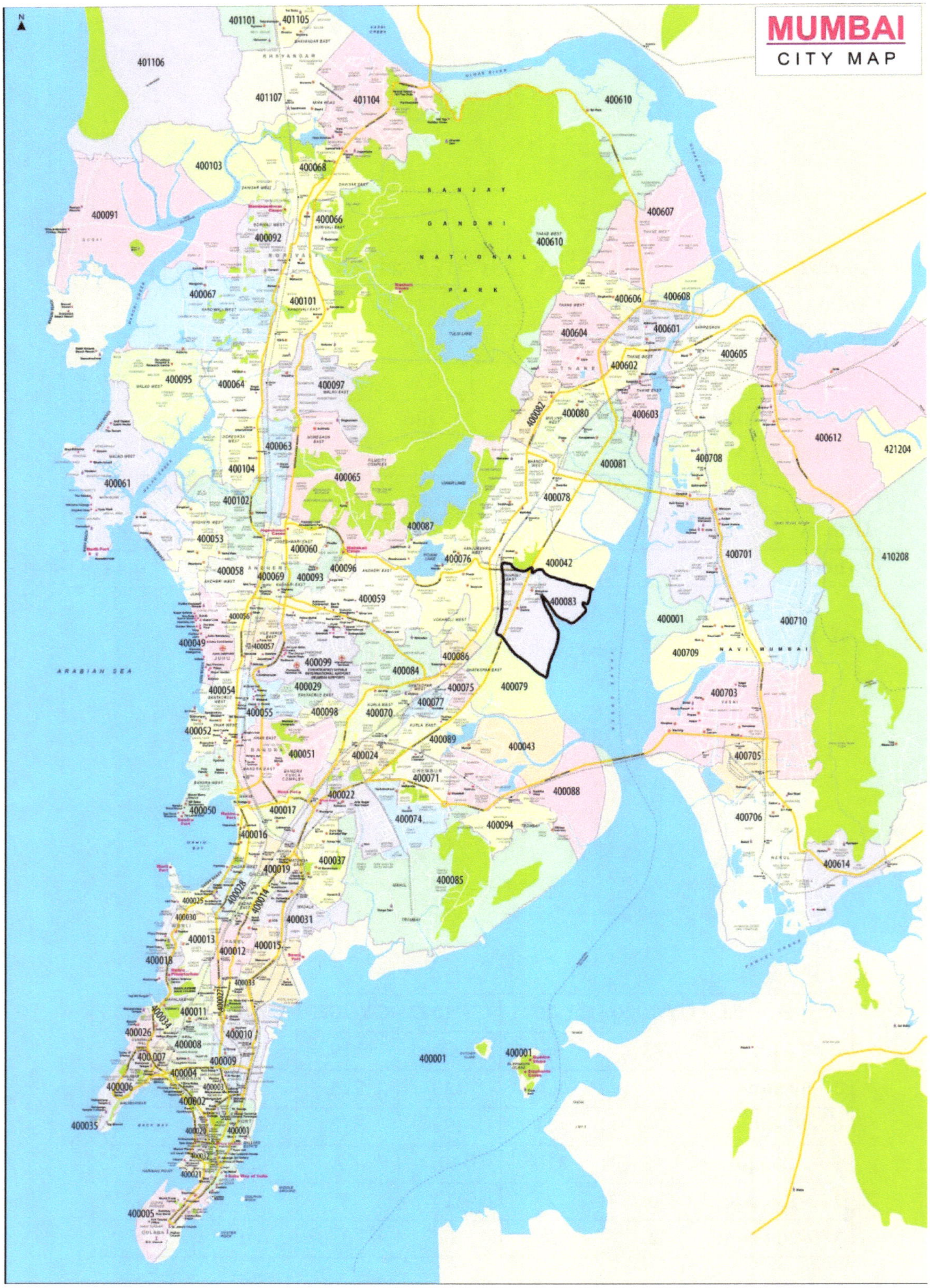

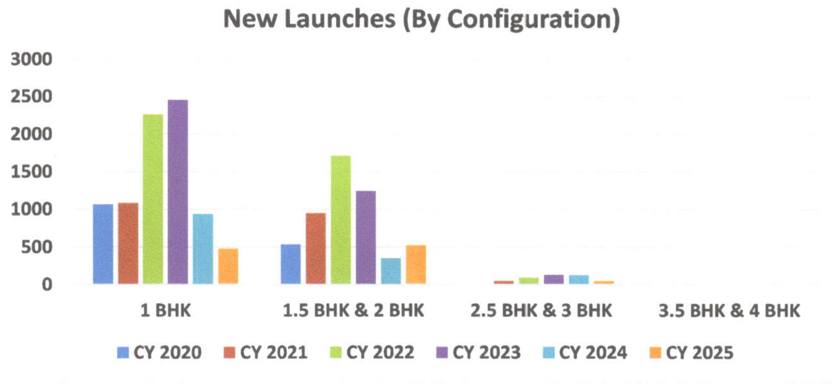

400083	CY 2020	CY 2021	CY 2022	CY 2023	CY 2024	CY 2025
Total Units	1788	2329	4239	4123	1750	1097
1 BHK	1068	1081	2254	2450	935	474
1.5 BHK & 2 BHK	538	948	1710	1243	352	521
2.5 BHK & 3 BHK	1	48	88	133	124	46
3.5 BHK & 4 BHK	0	0	0	0	0	0
Shops	83	85	108	156	55	35
Offices	10	14	46	21	226	4
Others	0	132	11	47	0	0

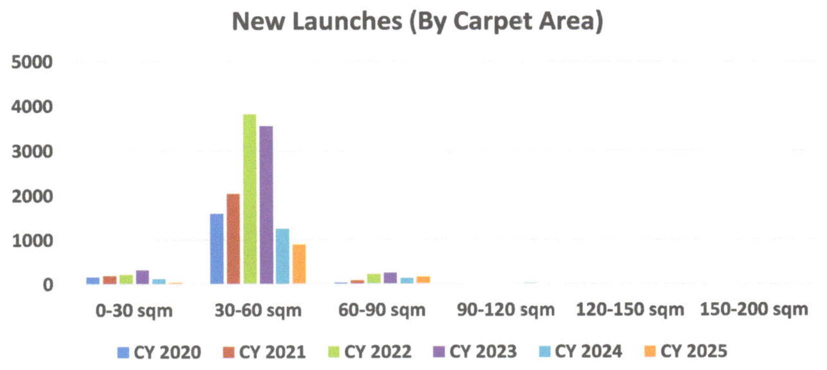

Carpet Area	CY 2020	CY 2021	CY 2022	CY 2023	CY 2024	CY 2025
0-30 sqm	162	190	207	314	116	34
30-60 sqm	1594	2042	3810	3547	1258	899
60-90 sqm	30	88	215	253	136	163
90-120 sqm	2	3	7	6	20	0
120-150 sqm	0	3	0	0	2	1
150-200 sqm	0	1	0	0	0	0

400086 (Ghatkopar West)

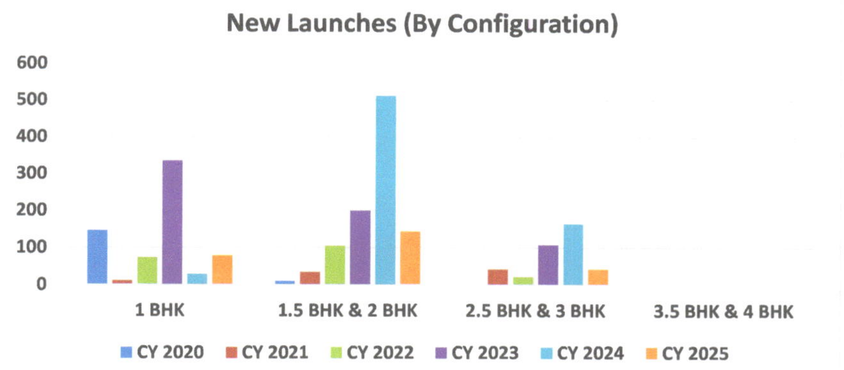

400086	CY 2020	CY 2021	CY 2022	CY 2023	CY 2024	CY 2025
Total Units	705	424	403	1136	895	309
1 BHK	145	11	72	335	28	78
1.5 BHK & 2 BHK	10	34	104	199	512	143
2.5 BHK & 3 BHK	0	42	21	108	164	42
3.5 BHK & 4 BHK	0	0	0	1	0	0
Shops	10	18	39	46	34	28
Offices	516	319	154	444	138	17
Others	19	0	0	3	1	0

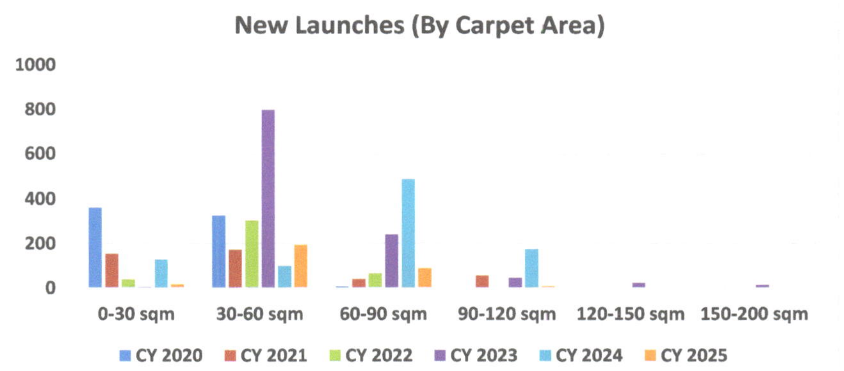

Carpet Area	CY 2020	CY 2021	CY 2022	CY 2023	CY 2024	CY 2025
0-30 sqm	362	153	36	5	129	16
30-60 sqm	325	172	302	798	99	193
60-90 sqm	8	40	64	241	487	88
90-120 sqm	1	56	0	46	175	8
120-150 sqm	2	2	0	24	2	1
150-200 sqm	3	1	0	14	1	2

400089 (Kurla/Lokmanya Tilak Terminus)

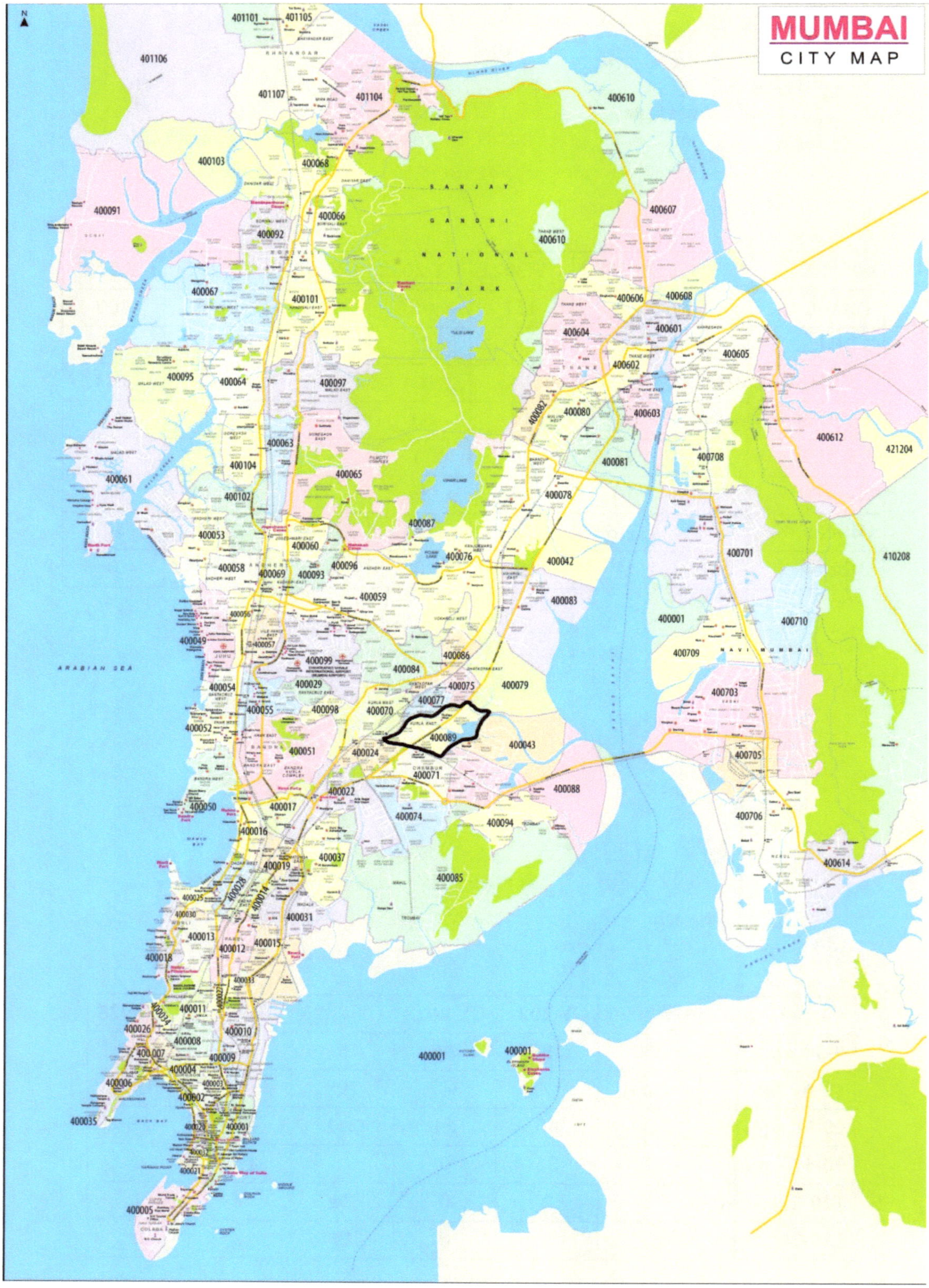

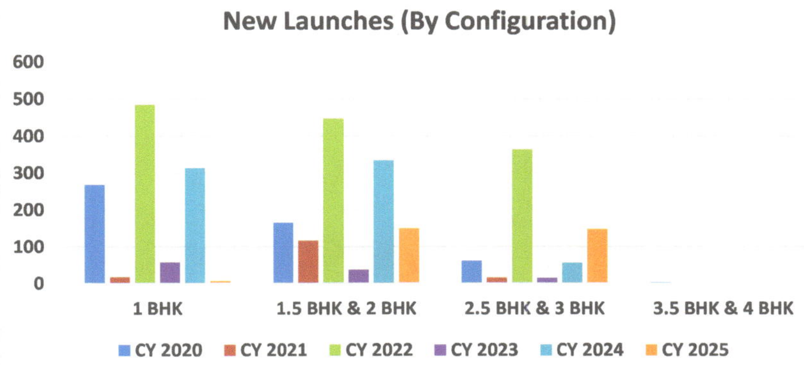

400089	CY 2020	CY 2021	CY 2022	CY 2023	CY 2024	CY 2025
Total Units	911	156	1380	108	782	417
1 BHK	267	17	483	57	313	6
1.5 BHK & 2 BHK	165	116	446	37	334	149
2.5 BHK & 3 BHK	61	15	363	14	55	147
3.5 BHK & 4 BHK	2	0	0	0	0	1
Shops	64	8	43	0	36	14
Offices	347	0	2	0	10	89
Others	5	0	27	0	21	11

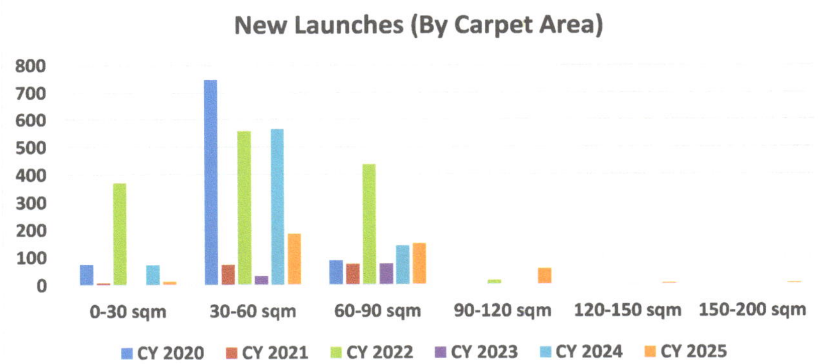

Carpet Area	CY 2020	CY 2021	CY 2022	CY 2023	CY 2024	CY 2025
0-30 sqm	75	8	370	0	72	12
30-60 sqm	748	73	557	32	566	185
60-90 sqm	88	75	436	76	142	148
90-120 sqm	0	0	15	0	1	57
120-150 sqm	0	0	1	0	0	5
150-200 sqm	0	0	1	0	1	6

400091 (Borivali West)

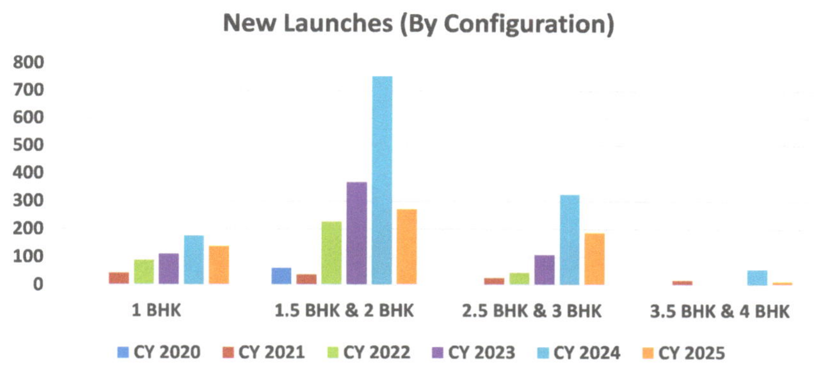

400091	CY 2020	CY 2021	CY 2022	CY 2023	CY 2024	CY 2025
Total Units	60	139	363	685	1483	702
1 BHK	0	43	87	111	176	138
1.5 BHK & 2 BHK	60	37	225	368	753	270
2.5 BHK & 3 BHK	0	24	42	108	324	186
3.5 BHK & 4 BHK	0	16	0	2	56	11
Shops	0	10	9	26	30	50
Offices	0	8	0	70	62	26
Others	0	0	0	0	66	20

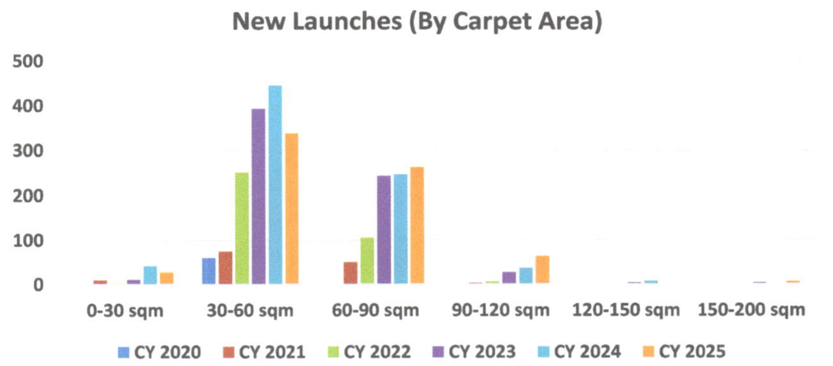

Carpet Area	CY 2020	CY 2021	CY 2022	CY 2023	CY 2024	CY 2025
0-30 sqm	0	9	2	11	42	27
30-60 sqm	60	75	250	393	446	338
60-90 sqm	0	50	105	243	246	262
90-120 sqm	0	3	6	27	37	63
120-150 sqm	0	1	0	4	7	0
150-200 sqm	0	1	0	4	0	6

400092 (Gorai/Borivali West)

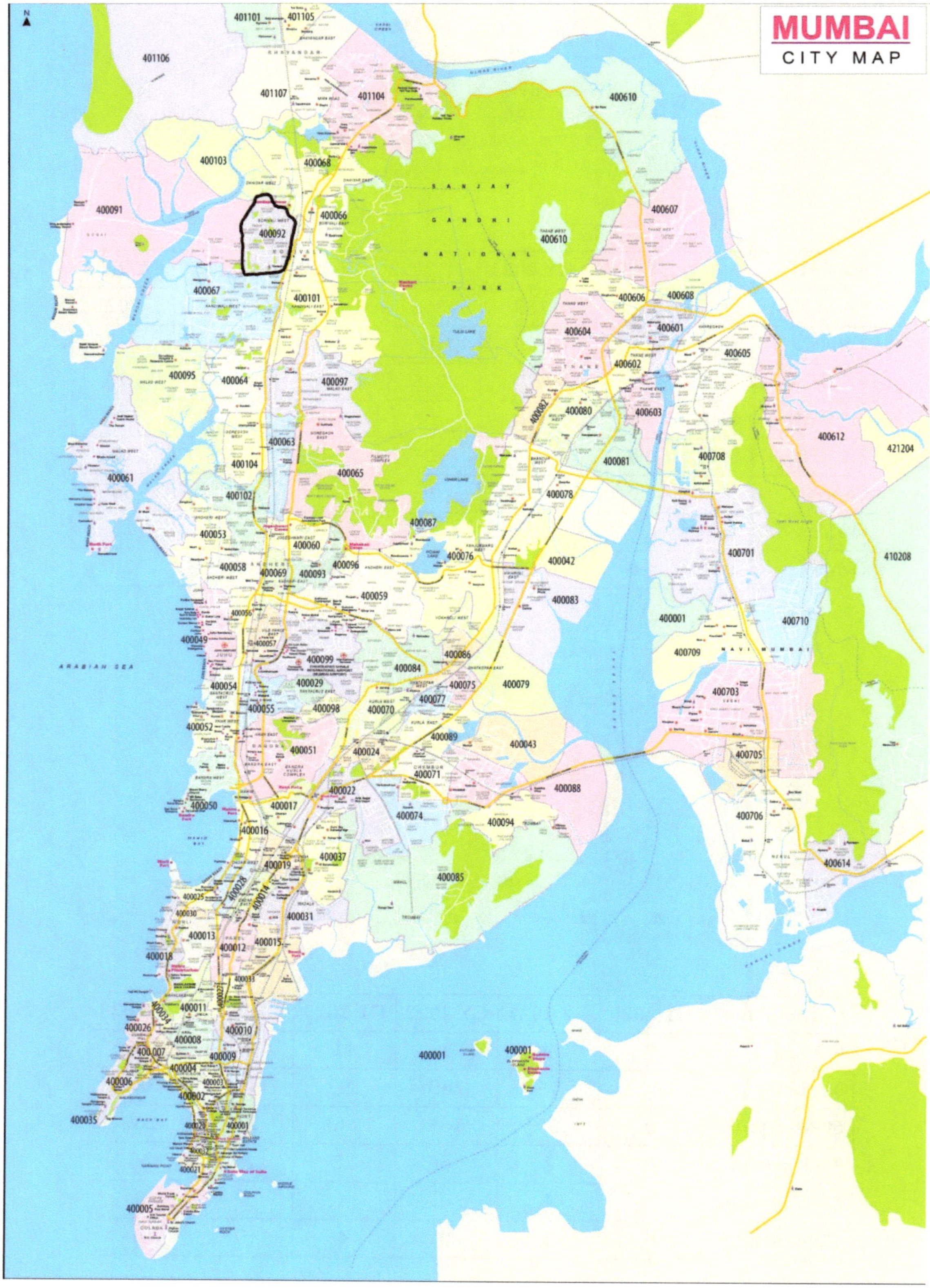

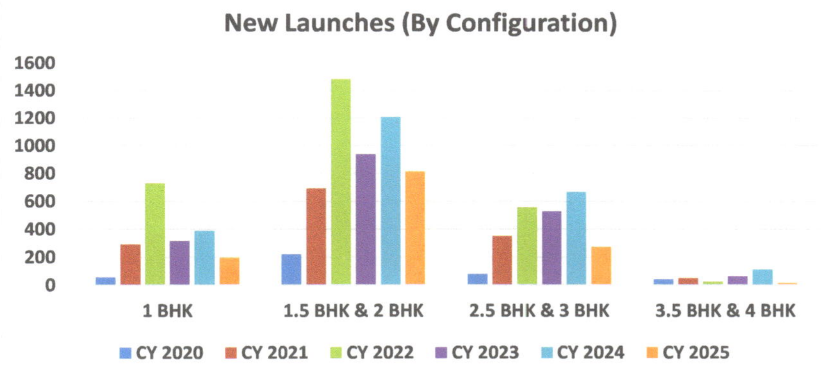

400092	CY 2020	CY 2021	CY 2022	CY 2023	CY 2024	CY 2025
Total Units	664	1781	3559	2283	3275	1593
1 BHK	56	291	726	315	388	196
1.5 BHK & 2 BHK	220	690	1481	939	1207	812
2.5 BHK & 3 BHK	79	350	555	528	667	270
3.5 BHK & 4 BHK	40	48	23	64	112	14
Shops	46	136	167	160	264	212
Offices	223	205	430	186	393	41
Others	0	44	109	19	74	43

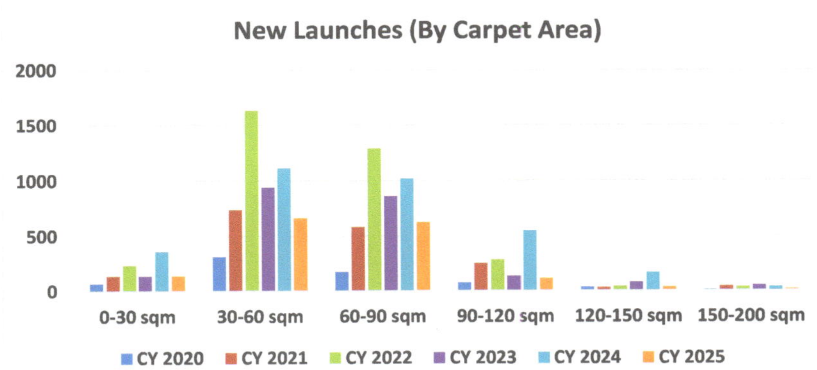

Carpet Area	CY 2020	CY 2021	CY 2022	CY 2023	CY 2024	CY 2025
0-30 sqm	68	135	233	136	359	136
30-60 sqm	311	739	1632	940	1111	663
60-90 sqm	171	581	1285	864	1018	623
90-120 sqm	74	251	280	134	547	112
120-150 sqm	31	27	37	76	165	32
150-200 sqm	9	39	33	49	35	11

400095 (Malvani/Marve)

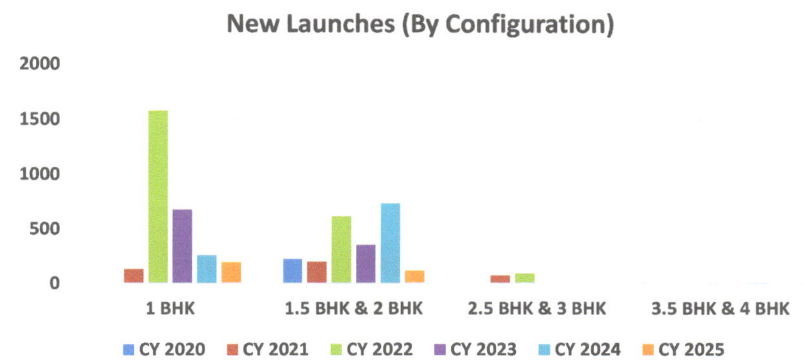

400095	CY 2020	CY 2021	CY 2022	CY 2023	CY 2024	CY 2025
Total Units	223	405	2340	1148	1062	315
1 BHK	0	129	1575	675	257	193
1.5 BHK & 2 BHK	223	198	612	351	735	115
2.5 BHK & 3 BHK	0	70	87	1	0	0
3.5 BHK & 4 BHK	0	0	0	0	9	0
Shops	0	5	54	44	26	4
Offices	0	0	10	6	8	3
Others	0	3	1	71	27	0

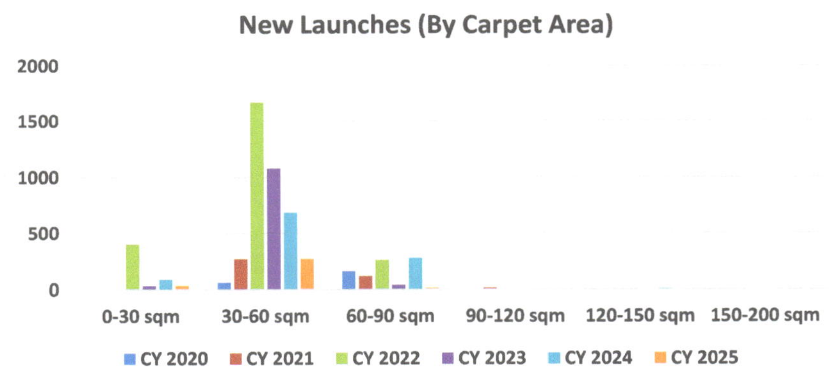

Carpet Area	CY 2020	CY 2021	CY 2022	CY 2023	CY 2024	CY 2025
0-30 sqm	0	6	400	32	88	34
30-60 sqm	63	271	1668	1078	685	270
60-90 sqm	160	115	257	38	278	11
90-120 sqm	0	12	0	0	2	0
120-150 sqm	0	0	3	0	9	0
150-200 sqm	0	0	1	0	0	0

400097 (Malad East)

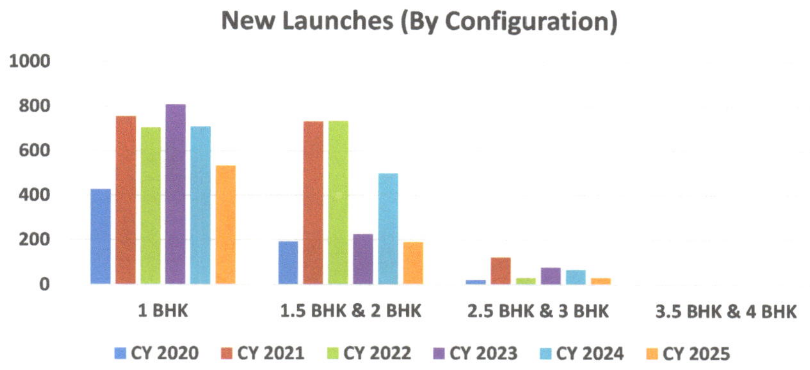

400097	CY 2020	CY 2021	CY 2022	CY 2023	CY 2024	CY 2025
Total Units	743	1796	1799	1533	2376	841
1 BHK	427	755	703	808	710	533
1.5 BHK & 2 BHK	192	733	734	225	499	190
2.5 BHK & 3 BHK	21	121	30	77	68	31
3.5 BHK & 4 BHK	0	1	0	2	0	0
Shops	1	21	242	116	107	42
Offices	47	149	14	294	862	7
Others	1	11	39	10	65	33

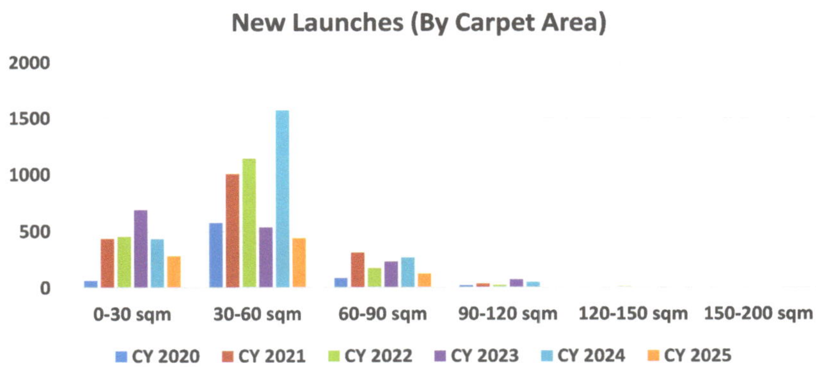

Carpet Area	CY 2020	CY 2021	CY 2022	CY 2023	CY 2024	CY 2025
0-30 sqm	63	435	453	692	432	278
30-60 sqm	574	1004	1139	535	1571	437
60-90 sqm	84	310	167	229	265	120
90-120 sqm	21	34	22	70	49	4
120-150 sqm	0	5	10	2	3	1
150-200 sqm	1	0	3	0	3	0

400101 (Kandivali East)

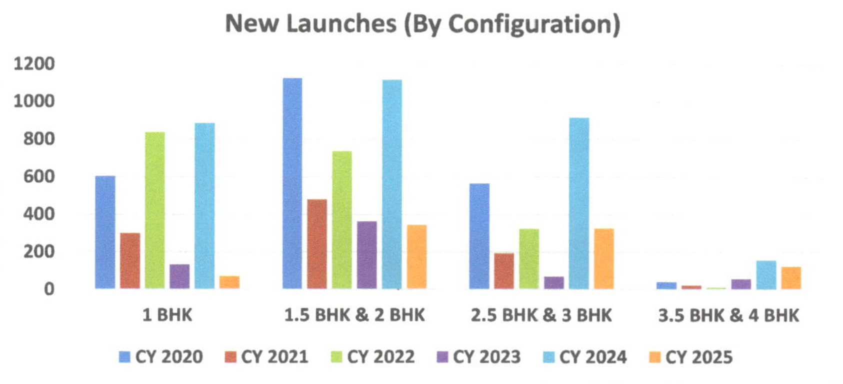

400101	CY 2020	CY 2021	CY 2022	CY 2023	CY 2024	CY 2025
Total Units	2407	1048	1979	684	3124	975
1 BHK	604	300	836	133	885	71
1.5 BHK & 2 BHK	1126	479	736	362	1118	342
2.5 BHK & 3 BHK	566	191	323	68	917	327
3.5 BHK & 4 BHK	41	22	11	56	157	122
Shops	46	13	8	18	43	113
Offices	0	40	2	42	0	0
Others	6	2	26	5	2	0

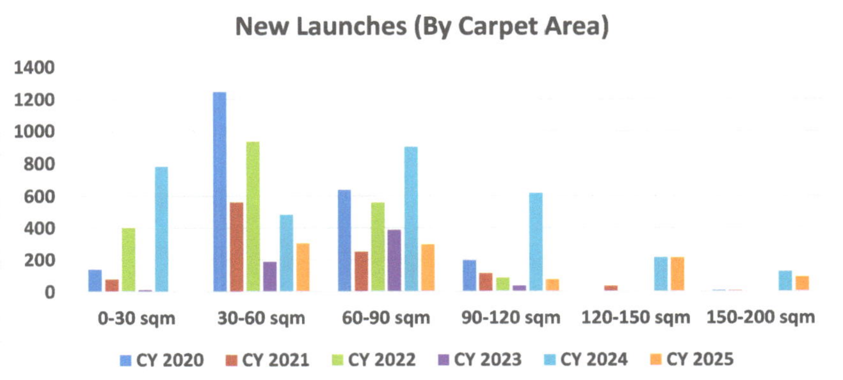

Carpet Area	CY 2020	CY 2021	CY 2022	CY 2023	CY 2024	CY 2025
0-30 sqm	139	77	400	12	783	0
30-60 sqm	1248	562	934	186	484	302
60-90 sqm	640	249	558	387	902	292
90-120 sqm	194	112	83	36	617	74
120-150 sqm	4	35	0	0	211	210
150-200 sqm	9	7	4	2	123	88

400102 (Oshiwara/Jogeshwari West)

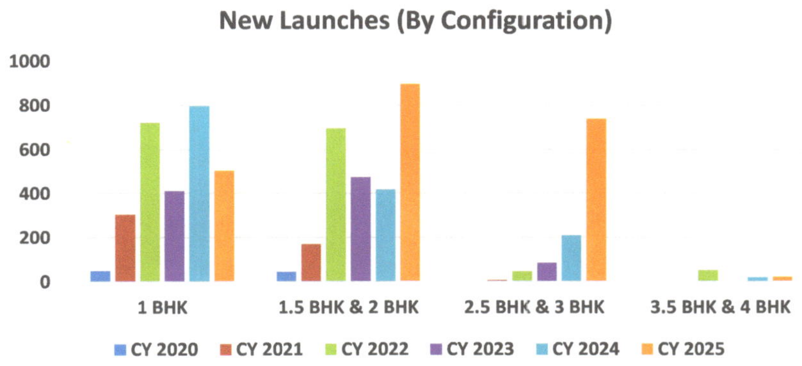

400102	CY 2020	CY 2021	CY 2022	CY 2023	CY 2024	CY 2025
Total Units	112	538	1640	1364	1567	2395
1 BHK	48	304	721	411	797	503
1.5 BHK & 2 BHK	45	169	696	474	419	896
2.5 BHK & 3 BHK	0	6	45	85	209	739
3.5 BHK & 4 BHK	0	0	50	0	19	21
Shops	3	25	50	75	86	168
Offices	0	18	56	315	7	30
Others	0	1	19	4	30	28

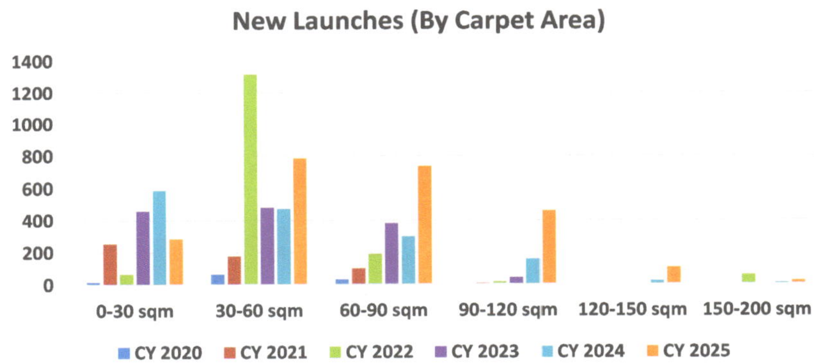

Carpet Area	CY 2020	CY 2021	CY 2022	CY 2023	CY 2024	CY 2025
0-30 sqm	16	254	64	459	589	284
30-60 sqm	64	175	1314	479	472	786
60-90 sqm	32	99	188	379	298	736
90-120 sqm	0	7	13	42	156	456
120-150 sqm	0	1	4	1	19	103
150-200 sqm	0	1	55	0	9	19

400103 (Mandapeshwar)

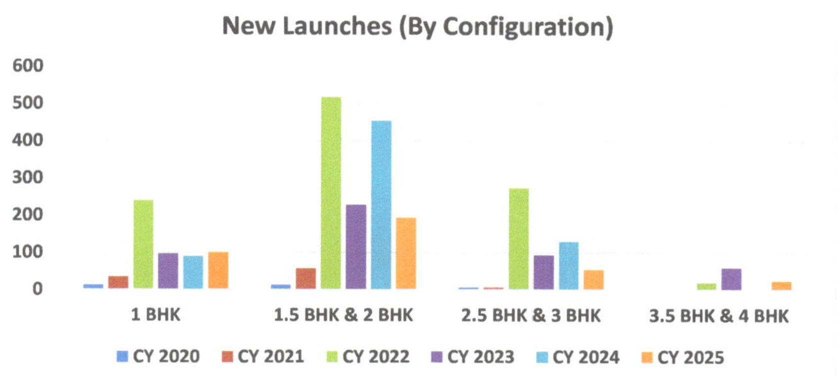

400103	CY 2020	CY 2021	CY 2022	CY 2023	CY 2024	CY 2025
Total Units	32	98	1205	531	803	489
1 BHK	13	35	239	97	90	100
1.5 BHK & 2 BHK	12	57	517	228	455	193
2.5 BHK & 3 BHK	6	6	273	93	129	54
3.5 BHK & 4 BHK	0	0	19	60	0	23
Shops	1	0	54	28	82	53
Offices	0	0	9	3	16	27
Others	0	0	85	18	26	36

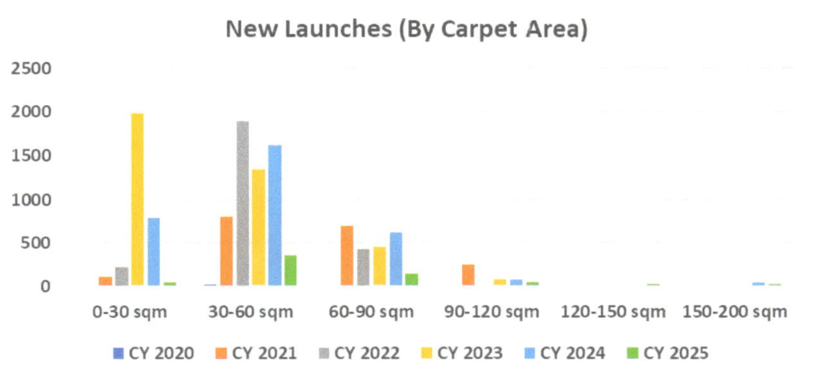

Carpet Area	CY 2020	CY 2021	CY 2022	CY 2023	CY 2024	CY 2025
0-30 sqm	1	0	42	26	62	54
30-60 sqm	25	69	617	249	283	229
60-90 sqm	6	29	380	180	380	145
90-120 sqm	0	0	146	13	72	32
120-150 sqm	0	0	6	0	1	2
150-200 sqm	0	0	5	30	2	4

400104 (Motilal Nagar)

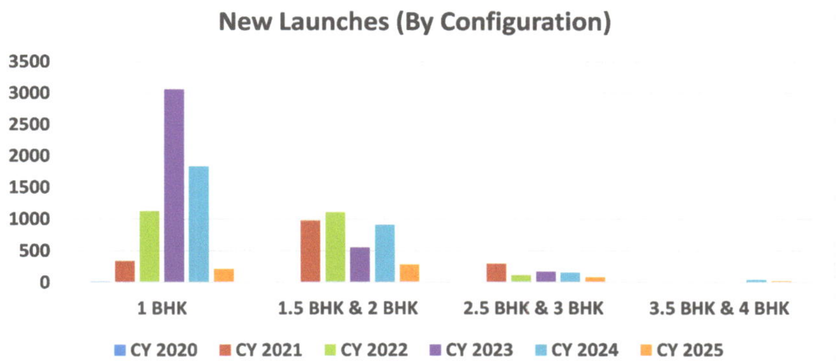

400104	CY 2020	CY 2021	CY 2022	CY 2023	CY 2024	CY 2025
Total Units	20	1869	2571	3855	3168	628
1 BHK	14	343	1116	3058	1831	212
1.5 BHK & 2 BHK	6	973	1100	556	912	282
2.5 BHK & 3 BHK	0	298	112	173	154	79
3.5 BHK & 4 BHK	0	2	5	11	45	21
Shops	0	80	181	16	68	27
Offices	0	113	17	7	18	1
Others	0	21	15	20	116	4

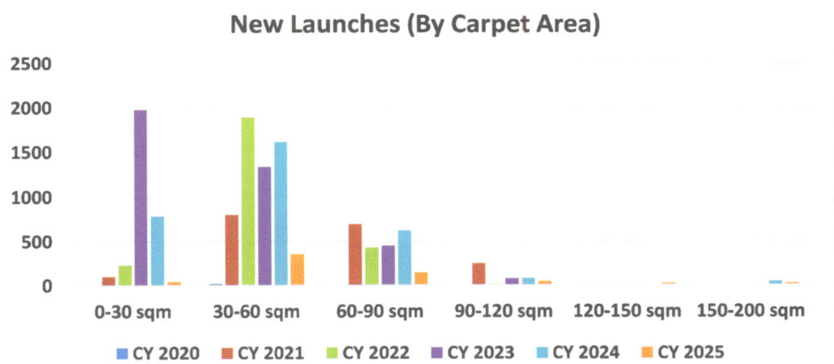

Carpet Area	CY 2020	CY 2021	CY 2022	CY 2023	CY 2024	CY 2025
0-30 sqm	0	102	227	1981	791	42
30-60 sqm	19	804	1890	1337	1616	355
60-90 sqm	1	697	428	449	626	143
90-120 sqm	0	250	10	76	77	43
120-150 sqm	0	0	6	3	8	22
150-200 sqm	0	1	6	4	45	21

Annexures

Total New Supply in Mumbai City over the years						
		CY 2021	CY 2022	CY 2023	CY 2024	CY 2025
New Launches in Mumbai City	units	54,736	76,472	66,941	70,892	42,643

Carpet Area		**CY 2021**	**CY 2022**	**CY 2023**	**CY 2024**	**CY 2025**
0-30 sqm	units	7,538	7,675	9,026	8,294	5,372
30-60 sqm	units	30,374	40,279	31,614	30,161	16,675
60-90 sqm	units	10,793	18,590	16,786	19,185	11,606
90-120 sqm	units	3,439	5,820	5,178	7,366	4,637
% units < 60 sqm carpet area	%	69%	63%	61%	54%	52%
% units 60-120 sqm carpet area	%	26%	32%	33%	37%	38%
% units > 120 sqm carpet area	%	5%	5%	6%	8%	10%
Avg. carpet area per unit	sqm	55.9	60.0	60.7	63.5	69.3

Configuration		**CY 2021**	**CY 2022**	**CY 2023**	**CY 2024**	**CY 2025**
1 RK & Studio	units	1,518	1,129	1,704	832	790
1 BHK	units	19,691	22,799	21,192	19,281	9,786
1.5 BHK & 2 BHK	units	20,237	28,793	23,251	26,021	14,485
2.5 BHK & 3 BHK	units	6,110	12,066	9,847	12,044	8,263
3.5 BHK & 4 BHK	units	1,000	1,678	1,878	2,320	1,826
Office	units	2,555	5,439	4,753	4,816	3,059
Shop	units	2,106	2,632	2,541	2,926	2,597
1 BHK	%	36%	30%	32%	27%	23%
1.5 BHK & 2 BHK	%	37%	38%	35%	37%	34%
2.5 BHK & 3 BHK	%	11%	16%	15%	17%	19%
3.5 BHK & 4 BHK	%	2%	2%	3%	3%	4%
Trivia		**CY 2021**	**CY 2022**	**CY 2023**	**CY 2024**	**CY 2025**
New Project Registrations		559	912	726	731	689
Active Projects		151	324	540	699	687
Lapsed Projects		181	283	122	25	1

Completed Projects		227	305	64	7	1
Projects with Excavation Completed		486	810	613	491	209
Projects with RCC Completed		350	562	285	100	5
Projects with Finishing Completed		232	297	78	16	1
Total Building Count	nos	711	1,095	942	984	902
Avg. Building Floors per Project		19.7	19.5	17.3	16.5	14.8

Total New Supply in Mumbai City over the years						
New Supply in selected micro markets	**Pin Code**	**CY 2021**	**CY 2022**	**CY 2023**	**CY 2024**	**CY 2025**
Kalbadevi	400002	312	124	250	222	5
Girgaon	400004	9	732	678	224	411
Mumbai Central	400008	341	618	719	499	596
Mazgaon Dock	400010	210	101	824	177	158
Byculla West	400011	483	1,200	568	172	763
Parel	400012	395	652	434	884	50
Lower Parel	400013	499	269	-	492	583
Dadar East	400014	-	336	467	372	252
Mahim/Matunga West	400016	946	799	208	421	1,229
Matunga	400019	112	473	241	292	418
Sion	400022	1,053	1,334	869	1,211	1,157
Kurla East	400024	995	1,426	832	1,317	152
Prabhadevi	400025	227	187	-	98	92
Dadar West	400028	395	640	187	733	349
Wadala	400031	61	702	400	362	70
Cotton Green	400033	217	543	-	194	61
Antop Hill	400037	1,052	543	242	248	239
Bhandup East	400042	844	1,567	857	643	57
Deonar/Govandi West	400043	596	1,124	17	-	88
Juhu	400049	133	492	271	252	600
Bandra West	400050	336	655	476	805	886
Bandra East	400051	546	897	1,349	722	1,048
Khar West	400052	84	423	377	536	481
Andheri-Azad Nagar	400053	1,437	1,508	987	1,092	1,216
Santacruz West	400054	835	729	519	417	599
Santacruz East	400055	420	516	540	412	574
Vile Parle West	400056	84	263	434	419	878
Vile Parle East	400057	353	896	844	1,357	730
Andheri West	400058	864	760	696	1,160	976
Andheri East-Marol	400059	899	444	2,014	1,224	728
Jogeshwari East	400060	644	2,478	2,017	404	216
Madh-Versova	400061	-	494	330	159	309
Goregaon West	400062	357	630	132	36	246
Goregaon East	400063	1,224	1,151	1,256	1,811	1,152
Malad West	400064	1,927	2,576	2,692	4,478	1,968
Borivali East	400066	1,224	4,753	2,284	3,026	1,066
Kandivali West	400067	2,778	2,818	4,300	1,640	1,605

Dahisar	400068	3,121	1,352	1,107	1,676	952
Andheri East	400069	616	438	1,812	254	328
Kurla West	400070	634	148	283	610	421
Chembur	400071	1,459	1,344	2,096	1,758	1,088
Saki Naka-Chandivali	400072	2,118	1,438	892	643	917
Mahul	400074	387	73	314	2,175	248
Ghatkopar East	400075	2,696	2,792	1,124	634	385
Powai	400076	447	769	426	773	410
Ghatkopar East	400077	965	882	973	1,897	613
Bhandup West	400078	3,581	1,986	2,339	4,227	954
Vikhroli	400079	-	1,384	271	1,026	-
Mulund West	400080	1,380	3,754	3,719	2,478	1,737
Mulund East	400081	988	719	1,930	1,296	688
Vikhroli	400083	2,329	4,239	4,123	1,750	1,097
Ghatkopar West	400086	424	403	1,136	895	309
Deonar-Mankhurd	400088	641	127	319	205	55
Lokmanya Tilak Terminus	400089	156	1,380	108	782	417
Borivali West	400091	139	363	685	1,483	702
Borivali West-Gorai	400092	1,781	3,559	2,283	3,275	1,593
Andheri East-Chakala	400093	644	543	388	107	143
Malvani-Marve	400095	405	2,340	1,148	1,062	315
Malad East	400097	1,796	1,799	1,533	2,376	841
Santacruz East	400098	86	119	466	275	192
Mumbai Airport	400099	-	401	69	298	61
Kandivali East	400101	1,048	1,979	684	3,124	975
Jogeshwari West-Oshiwara	400102	538	1,640	1,364	1,567	2,395
Mandapeshwar	400103	98	1,205	531	803	489
Motilal Nagar	400104	1,869	2,571	3,855	3,168	628
TOTAL		**53,238**	**75,600**	**65,289**	**69,128**	**40,961**
Market Share in Mumbai City		97%	99%	98%	98%	96%

Total New Supply over the years (0 - 30 sqm MahaRERA Carpet Area)						
New Supply in selected micro markets	**Pin Code**	**CY 2021**	**CY 2022**	**CY 2023**	**CY 2024**	**CY 2025**
Kalbadevi	400002	1	4	15	172	5
Girgaon	400004	4	53	52	68	91
Mumbai Central	400008	23	23	56	98	85
Mazgaon Dock	400010	-	5	36	8	12
Byculla West	400011	25	-	9	96	97
Parel	400012	54	12	23	63	5
Lower Parel	400013	153	109	-	16	6
Dadar East	400014	-	3	31	19	16
Mahim/Matunga West	400016	11	47	12	30	43
Matunga	400019	3	8	12	6	33
Sion	400022	864	8	54	155	8
Kurla East	400024	144	37	17	192	3
Prabhadevi	400025	-	-	-	1	-
Dadar West	400028	28	110	1	179	12
Wadala	400031	61	4	7	-	3
Cotton Green	400033	-	2	-	13	2
Antop Hill	400037	1	9	70	-	-
Bhandup East	400042	14	33	107	135	1
Deonar/Govandi West	400043	268	831	-	-	-
Juhu	400049	-	13	-	-	427
Bandra West	400050	44	8	12	125	130
Bandra East	400051	341	209	306	6	-
Khar West	400052	2	26	7	102	45
Andheri-Azad Nagar	400053	93	7	55	-	5
Santacruz West	400054	64	16	18	18	190
Santacruz East	400055	65	30	54	17	154
Vile Parle West	400056	3	38	47	34	32
Vile Parle East	400057	33	170	122	185	127
Andheri West	400058	101	57	25	109	91
Andheri East-Marol	400059	40	19	681	26	18
Jogeshwari East	400060	17	615	100	3	62
Madh-Versova	400061	-	-	20	-	1
Goregaon West	400062	118	35	6	9	22
Goregaon East	400063	94	32	21	234	216
Malad West	400064	171	134	279	281	569
Borivali East	400066	185	328	265	113	154
Kandivali West	400067	209	259	489	331	262

Dahisar	400068	154	179	87	367	152
Andheri East	400069	172	23	188	14	48
Kurla West	400070	220	20	18	182	111
Chembur	400071	43	46	709	118	66
Saki Naka-Chandivali	400072	69	35	18	3	130
Mahul	400074	24	-	16	73	-
Ghatkopar East	400075	51	178	69	66	116
Powai	400076	-	3	9	-	1
Ghatkopar East	400077	223	82	123	99	46
Bhandup West	400078	994	658	535	303	330
Vikhroli	400079	-	172	-	1	-
Mulund West	400080	384	213	362	340	310
Mulund East	400081	55	51	119	213	130
Vikhroli	400083	190	207	314	116	34
Ghatkopar West	400086	153	36	5	129	16
Deonar-Mankhurd	400088	110	2	3	9	-
Lokmanya Tilak Terminus	400089	8	370	-	72	12
Borivali West	400091	9	2	11	42	27
Borivali West-Gorai	400092	135	233	136	359	136
Andheri East-Chakala	400093	197	212	9	-	32
Malvani-Marve	400095	6	400	32	88	34
Malad East	400097	435	453	692	432	278
Santacruz East	400098	8	2	1	37	1
Mumbai Airport	400099	-	66	1	80	24
Kandivali East	400101	77	400	12	783	-
Jogeshwari West-Oshiwara	400102	254	64	459	589	284
Mandapeshwar	400103	-	42	26	62	54
Motilal Nagar	400104	102	227	1,981	791	42
TOTAL		**7,307**	**7,670**	**8,944**	**8,212**	**5,341**

Total New Supply over the years (30 - 60 sqm MahaRERA Carpet Area)						
New Supply in selected micro markets	**Pin Code**	**CY 2021**	**CY 2022**	**CY 2023**	**CY 2024**	**CY 2025**
Kalbadevi	400002	258	94	103	-	-
Girgaon	400004	1	314	416	134	140
Mumbai Central	400008	243	504	519	377	454
Mazgaon Dock	400010	210	59	481	168	103
Byculla West	400011	208	28	482	56	363
Parel	400012	338	5	195	382	43
Lower Parel	400013	140	119	-	98	162
Dadar East	400014	-	74	171	248	93
Mahim/Matunga West	400016	628	174	145	80	350
Matunga	400019	40	190	23	116	139
Sion	400022	113	738	140	277	139
Kurla East	400024	761	1,165	757	1,016	96
Prabhadevi	400025	17	162	-	58	63
Dadar West	400028	271	305	45	231	212
Wadala	400031	-	213	40	8	21
Cotton Green	400033	217	9	-	178	45
Antop Hill	400037	506	9	172	-	3
Bhandup East	400042	724	1,275	677	198	30
Deonar/Govandi West	400043	328	293	11	-	33
Juhu	400049	-	10	32	3	24
Bandra West	400050	113	87	135	164	49
Bandra East	400051	38	520	580	326	244
Khar West	400052	5	111	132	77	50
Andheri-Azad Nagar	400053	783	474	352	471	719
Santacruz West	400054	484	99	96	86	110
Santacruz East	400055	279	300	198	206	210
Vile Parle West	400056	18	50	107	36	181
Vile Parle East	400057	132	265	242	377	152
Andheri West	400058	441	322	461	435	437
Andheri East-Marol	400059	387	258	803	638	291
Jogeshwari East	400060	549	1,416	1,567	209	132
Madh-Versova	400061	-	452	24	7	7
Goregaon West	400062	143	199	37	27	132
Goregaon East	400063	389	722	463	694	385
Malad West	400064	1,226	1,586	1,252	2,311	830
Borivali East	400066	632	3,071	629	1,757	486
Kandivali West	400067	1,359	1,698	1,823	782	625

Dahisar	400068	2,475	941	752	915	648
Andheri East	400069	351	158	438	103	152
Kurla West	400070	348	110	202	360	195
Chembur	400071	1,129	558	618	1,127	396
Saki Naka-Chandivali	400072	1,399	670	666	206	335
Mahul	400074	198	65	28	1,626	2
Ghatkopar East	400075	1,407	1,572	757	306	121
Powai	400076	319	348	14	103	378
Ghatkopar East	400077	329	120	271	392	221
Bhandup West	400078	2,525	1,298	1,653	1,849	480
Vikhroli	400079	-	1,090	-	432	-
Mulund West	400080	695	492	1,187	561	562
Mulund East	400081	92	228	925	322	198
Vikhroli	400083	2,042	3,810	3,547	1,258	899
Ghatkopar West	400086	172	302	798	99	193
Deonar-Mankhurd	400088	128	22	135	92	26
Lokmanya Tilak Terminus	400089	73	557	32	566	185
Borivali West	400091	75	250	393	446	338
Borivali West-Gorai	400092	739	1,632	940	1,111	663
Andheri East-Chakala	400093	343	266	273	28	67
Malvani-Marve	400095	271	1,668	1,078	685	270
Malad East	400097	1,004	1,139	535	1,571	437
Santacruz East	400098	32	75	88	150	117
Mumbai Airport	400099	-	276	38	160	31
Kandivali East	400101	562	934	186	484	302
Jogeshwari West-Oshiwara	400102	175	1,314	479	472	786
Mandapeshwar	400103	69	617	249	283	229
Motilal Nagar	400104	804	1,890	1,337	1,616	355
TOTAL		**29,737**	**39,772**	**30,929**	**29,554**	**16,139**

Total New Supply over the years (60 - 90 sqm MahaRERA Carpet Area)						
New Supply in selected micro markets	**Pin Code**	**CY 2021**	**CY 2022**	**CY 2023**	**CY 2024**	**CY 2025**
Kalbadevi	400002	45	10	55	-	-
Girgaon	400004	4	228	149	19	90
Mumbai Central	400008	64	89	104	24	54
Mazgaon Dock	400010	-	32	253	1	36
Byculla West	400011	93	321	25	-	74
Parel	400012	2	333	174	247	-
Lower Parel	400013	9	25	-	168	59
Dadar East	400014	-	227	258	77	74
Mahim/Matunga West	400016	112	322	31	134	566
Matunga	400019	37	113	65	87	146
Sion	400022	48	289	222	485	688
Kurla East	400024	29	220	54	70	52
Prabhadevi	400025	17	-	-	23	1
Dadar West	400028	65	125	40	159	115
Wadala	400031	-	312	242	228	20
Cotton Green	400033	-	321	-	2	-
Antop Hill	400037	414	269	-	244	113
Bhandup East	400042	99	232	61	-	26
Deonar/Govandi West	400043	-	-	6	-	25
Juhu	400049	7	19	35	9	52
Bandra West	400050	37	117	97	247	168
Bandra East	400051	89	116	401	296	255
Khar West	400052	19	154	106	168	154
Andheri-Azad Nagar	400053	396	356	240	201	279
Santacruz West	400054	167	211	202	118	175
Santacruz East	400055	70	160	209	154	110
Vile Parle West	400056	52	79	139	126	218
Vile Parle East	400057	131	288	338	540	360
Andheri West	400058	231	305	180	470	283
Andheri East-Marol	400059	442	139	260	338	211
Jogeshwari East	400060	71	400	322	186	4
Madh-Versova	400061	-	16	156	42	93
Goregaon West	400062	89	337	86	-	84
Goregaon East	400063	266	346	242	694	259
Malad West	400064	396	730	1,001	1,256	478
Borivali East	400066	60	925	897	907	286
Kandivali West	400067	876	597	1,568	422	582

Dahisar	400068	386	207	105	260	131
Andheri East	400069	67	215	792	130	108
Kurla West	400070	18	17	53	63	109
Chembur	400071	204	557	424	395	377
Saki Naka-Chandivali	400072	639	456	164	99	111
Mahul	400074	45	8	134	426	240
Ghatkopar East	400075	972	864	248	130	126
Powai	400076	128	89	48	558	31
Ghatkopar East	400077	274	320	292	645	194
Bhandup West	400078	57	22	146	1,551	72
Vikhroli	400079	-	85	5	344	-
Mulund West	400080	111	2,129	1,393	797	517
Mulund East	400081	461	385	832	533	269
Vikhroli	400083	88	215	253	136	163
Ghatkopar West	400086	40	64	241	487	88
Deonar-Mankhurd	400088	196	96	78	72	-
Lokmanya Tilak Terminus	400089	75	436	76	142	148
Borivali West	400091	50	105	243	246	262
Borivali West-Gorai	400092	581	1,285	864	1,018	623
Andheri East-Chakala	400093	66	39	66	73	40
Malvani-Marve	400095	115	257	38	278	11
Malad East	400097	310	167	229	265	120
Santacruz East	400098	46	42	272	42	57
Mumbai Airport	400099	-	38	30	55	6
Kandivali East	400101	249	558	387	902	292
Jogeshwari West-Oshiwara	400102	99	188	379	298	736
Mandapeshwar	400103	29	380	180	380	145
Motilal Nagar	400104	697	428	449	626	143
TOTAL		**10,440**	**18,415**	**16,639**	**19,093**	**11,309**

Total New Supply over the years (90 - 120 sqm MahaRERA Carpet Area)						
New Supply in selected micro markets	**Pin Code**	**CY 2021**	**CY 2022**	**CY 2023**	**CY 2024**	**CY 2025**
Kalbadevi	400002	8	16	1	-	-
Girgaon	400004	-	97	58	2	44
Mumbai Central	400008	5	1	20	-	2
Mazgaon Dock	400010	-	5	54	-	7
Byculla West	400011	80	401	39	-	99
Parel	400012	1	144	42	151	-
Lower Parel	400013	51	-	-	99	19
Dadar East	400014	-	28	5	22	37
Mahim/Matunga West	400016	33	255	17	109	204
Matunga	400019	26	86	57	34	55
Sion	400022	17	214	242	263	253
Kurla East	400024	-	3	2	37	-
Prabhadevi	400025	3	-	-	16	4
Dadar West	400028	25	73	66	89	8
Wadala	400031	-	160	35	126	8
Cotton Green	400033	-	190	-	1	4
Antop Hill	400037	87	256	-	-	82
Bhandup East	400042	7	25	12	-	-
Deonar/Govandi West	400043	-	-	-	-	2
Juhu	400049	91	187	44	40	48
Bandra West	400050	27	154	58	81	217
Bandra East	400051	10	24	23	71	272
Khar West	400052	21	66	59	119	118
Andheri-Azad Nagar	400053	109	451	276	311	146
Santacruz West	400054	22	196	142	119	96
Santacruz East	400055	4	3	75	18	55
Vile Parle West	400056	10	61	126	142	331
Vile Parle East	400057	46	126	91	219	82
Andheri West	400058	72	66	24	86	101
Andheri East-Marol	400059	4	11	124	131	75
Jogeshwari East	400060	1	45	23	2	9
Madh-Versova	400061	-	8	-	18	36
Goregaon West	400062	3	48	1	-	8
Goregaon East	400063	33	44	10	128	131
Malad West	400064	86	120	132	356	55
Borivali East	400066	245	145	400	239	70
Kandivali West	400067	284	87	330	62	116

Dahisar	400068	99	9	18	13	17
Andheri East	400069	8	40	183	5	17
Kurla West	400070	-	1	7	2	4
Chembur	400071	38	110	250	62	163
Saki Naka-Chandivali	400072	5	168	43	92	127
Mahul	400074	16	-	134	26	2
Ghatkopar East	400075	208	164	33	129	22
Powai	400076	-	303	281	102	-
Ghatkopar East	400077	126	215	122	529	124
Bhandup West	400078	5	2	3	456	25
Vikhroli	400079	-	21	248	189	-
Mulund West	400080	130	329	472	487	278
Mulund East	400081	316	29	49	222	40
Vikhroli	400083	3	7	6	20	-
Ghatkopar West	400086	56	-	46	175	8
Deonar-Mankhurd	400088	152	4	12	31	20
Lokmanya Tilak Terminus	400089	-	15	-	1	57
Borivali West	400091	3	6	27	37	63
Borivali West-Gorai	400092	251	280	134	547	112
Andheri East-Chakala	400093	24	25	14	-	1
Malvani-Marve	400095	12	-	-	2	-
Malad East	400097	34	22	70	49	4
Santacruz East	400098	-	-	51	33	16
Mumbai Airport	400099	-	2	-	3	-
Kandivali East	400101	112	83	36	617	74
Jogeshwari West-Oshiwara	400102	7	13	42	156	456
Mandapeshwar	400103	-	146	13	72	32
Motilal Nagar	400104	250	10	76	77	43
TOTAL		**3,266**	**5,800**	**4,958**	**7,225**	**4,499**

Total New Supply over the years (1 BHK)						
New Supply in selected micro markets	**Pin Code**	**CY 2021**	**CY 2022**	**CY 2023**	**CY 2024**	**CY 2025**
Kalbadevi	400002	101	33	20	2	-
Girgaon	400004	-	183	290	108	102
Mumbai Central	400008	178	413	400	255	355
Mazgaon Dock	400010	107	43	302	155	91
Byculla West	400011	177	28	219	122	152
Parel	400012	371	-	102	371	42
Lower Parel	400013	17	86	-	11	-
Dadar East	400014	-	22	164	154	66
Mahim/Matunga West	400016	391	123	92	51	264
Matunga	400019	35	170	11	68	28
Sion	400022	855	160	90	57	8
Kurla East	400024	442	687	454	617	52
Prabhadevi	400025	3	148	-	-	42
Dadar West	400028	198	181	31	267	143
Wadala	400031	-	116	24	8	1
Cotton Green	400033	213	9	-	134	34
Antop Hill	400037	192	-	61	-	-
Bhandup East	400042	327	372	296	450	8
Deonar/Govandi West	400043	398	875	-	-	-
Juhu	400049	-	3	17	4	368
Bandra West	400050	62	43	55	153	105
Bandra East	400051	390	109	381	1	2
Khar West	400052	1	30	74	121	9
Andheri-Azad Nagar	400053	378	154	179	436	166
Santacruz West	400054	-	46	26	51	243
Santacruz East	400055	254	243	105	64	77
Vile Parle West	400056	15	8	28	9	30
Vile Parle East	400057	84	143	118	253	157
Andheri West	400058	159	241	213	182	268
Andheri East-Marol	400059	331	143	406	172	247
Jogeshwari East	400060	239	1,162	638	168	126
Madh-Versova	400061	-	350	22	2	-
Goregaon West	400062	53	87	14	18	86
Goregaon East	400063	232	211	200	313	142
Malad West	400064	788	676	666	1,354	706
Borivali East	400066	414	1,129	464	831	266
Kandivali West	400067	824	818	1,063	265	420

Dahisar	400068	1,662	457	480	692	167
Andheri East	400069	170	77	370	61	135
Kurla West	400070	355	75	133	401	161
Chembur	400071	452	296	453	611	160
Saki Naka-Chandivali	400072	733	230	497	100	98
Mahul	400074	171	50	28	1,090	1
Ghatkopar East	400075	623	672	355	207	114
Powai	400076	93	175	-	95	200
Ghatkopar East	400077	156	72	79	111	3
Bhandup West	400078	2,418	1,262	1,321	917	462
Vikhroli	400079	-	109	-	-	-
Mulund West	400080	459	305	743	366	380
Mulund East	400081	26	186	612	366	126
Vikhroli	400083	1,081	2,254	2,450	935	474
Ghatkopar West	400086	11	72	335	28	78
Deonar-Mankhurd	400088	-	3	102	74	26
Lokmanya Tilak Terminus	400089	17	483	57	313	6
Borivali West	400091	43	87	111	176	138
Borivali West-Gorai	400092	291	726	315	388	196
Andheri East-Chakala	400093	266	323	89	-	31
Malvani-Marve	400095	129	1,575	675	257	193
Malad East	400097	755	703	808	710	533
Santacruz East	400098	18	46	49	20	108
Mumbai Airport	400099	-	89	20	133	14
Kandivali East	400101	300	836	133	885	71
Jogeshwari West-Oshiwara	400102	304	721	411	797	503
Mandapeshwar	400103	35	239	97	90	100
Motilal Nagar	400104	343	1,116	3,058	1,831	212
TOTAL		**19,140**	**22,484**	**21,006**	**18,881**	**9,496**

Total New Supply over the years (2 BHK)						
New Supply in selected micro markets	**Pin Code**	**CY 2021**	**CY 2022**	**CY 2023**	**CY 2024**	**CY 2025**
Kalbadevi	400002	157	63	98	-	-
Girgaon	400004	4	209	209	33	92
Mumbai Central	400008	104	155	182	141	114
Mazgaon Dock	400010	102	35	338	10	39
Byculla West	400011	105	168	281	-	244
Parel	400012	14	324	274	252	-
Lower Parel	400013	-	22	-	193	164
Dadar East	400014	-	260	270	155	71
Mahim/Matunga West	400016	464	338	75	175	444
Matunga	400019	15	109	47	97	235
Sion	400022	78	607	188	471	729
Kurla East	400024	387	649	287	547	92
Prabhadevi	400025	13	-	-	16	19
Dadar West	400028	116	191	42	201	153
Wadala	400031	-	312	168	228	20
Cotton Green	400033	4	181	-	41	13
Antop Hill	400037	727	270	172	122	108
Bhandup East	400042	374	653	407	176	33
Deonar/Govandi West	400043	172	249	11	-	-
Juhu	400049	6	25	36	9	51
Bandra West	400050	16	108	68	267	70
Bandra East	400051	98	516	480	500	252
Khar West	400052	3	101	132	102	124
Andheri-Azad Nagar	400053	620	432	307	224	703
Santacruz West	400054	121	137	230	101	145
Santacruz East	400055	112	216	232	247	101
Vile Parle West	400056	33	114	166	79	285
Vile Parle East	400057	141	281	313	484	312
Andheri West	400058	320	363	288	520	359
Andheri East-Marol	400059	376	217	593	326	236
Jogeshwari East	400060	354	794	912	141	60
Madh-Versova	400061	-	119	178	10	76
Goregaon West	400062	185	240	81	9	102
Goregaon East	400063	176	402	307	778	259
Malad West	400064	744	1,149	1,244	1,609	561
Borivali East	400066	284	1,875	858	1,673	379
Kandivali West	400067	1,197	1,197	1,623	570	612

Dahisar	400068	1,252	465	516	799	547
Andheri East	400069	238	248	678	146	46
Kurla West	400070	110	60	123	104	105
Chembur	400071	857	613	586	738	376
Saki Naka-Chandivali	400072	934	601	275	44	33
Mahul	400074	76	22	133	691	239
Ghatkopar East	400075	1,663	1,606	586	213	149
Powai	400076	226	209	52	629	176
Ghatkopar East	400077	197	300	206	437	118
Bhandup West	400078	585	480	566	2,110	214
Vikhroli	400079	-	345	5	650	-
Mulund West	400080	692	1,372	1,321	673	572
Mulund East	400081	504	356	1,025	508	329
Vikhroli	400083	948	1,710	1,243	352	521
Ghatkopar West	400086	34	104	199	512	143
Deonar-Mankhurd	400088	238	63	60	50	-
Lokmanya Tilak Terminus	400089	116	446	37	334	149
Borivali West	400091	37	225	368	753	270
Borivali West-Gorai	400092	690	1,481	939	1,207	812
Andheri East-Chakala	400093	13	107	182	-	63
Malvani-Marve	400095	198	612	351	735	115
Malad East	400097	733	734	225	499	190
Santacruz East	400098	39	64	213	17	48
Mumbai Airport	400099	-	80	43	127	16
Kandivali East	400101	479	736	362	1,118	342
Jogeshwari West-Oshiwara	400102	169	696	474	419	896
Mandapeshwar	400103	57	517	228	455	193
Motilal Nagar	400104	973	1,100	556	912	282
TOTAL		**19,680**	**28,433**	**22,649**	**25,739**	**14,201**

Total New Supply over the years (3 BHK)						
New Supply in selected micro markets	**Pin Code**	**CY 2021**	**CY 2022**	**CY 2023**	**CY 2024**	**CY 2025**
Kalbadevi	400002	51	20	-	-	-
Girgaon	400004	-	134	82	3	58
Mumbai Central	400008	8	22	64	1	10
Mazgaon Dock	400010	1	14	112	1	7
Byculla West	400011	114	624	39	-	143
Parel	400012	-	236	45	153	-
Lower Parel	400013	51	2	-	102	131
Dadar East	400014	-	30	7	19	41
Mahim/Matunga West	400016	62	266	20	143	216
Matunga	400019	45	118	144	70	103
Sion	400022	21	447	286	348	336
Kurla East	400024	26	46	54	87	-
Prabhadevi	400025	33	-	-	11	3
Dadar West	400028	39	102	94	135	10
Wadala	400031	-	162	196	126	26
Cotton Green	400033	-	331	-	-	8
Antop Hill	400037	88	254	-	122	78
Bhandup East	400042	89	207	37	-	15
Deonar/Govandi West	400043	-	-	6	-	-
Juhu	400049	101	274	165	111	72
Bandra West	400050	59	220	39	140	344
Bandra East	400051	-	47	195	188	392
Khar West	400052	25	90	105	92	194
Andheri-Azad Nagar	400053	187	657	372	337	297
Santacruz West	400054	60	301	177	162	144
Santacruz East	400055	17	19	140	51	56
Vile Parle West	400056	28	88	153	157	391
Vile Parle East	400057	74	231	214	343	181
Andheri West	400058	182	122	74	275	219
Andheri East-Marol	400059	101	55	121	147	157
Jogeshwari East	400060	18	147	141	90	-
Madh-Versova	400061	-	18	90	34	129
Goregaon West	400062	29	222	31	-	28
Goregaon East	400063	295	122	367	200	148
Malad West	400064	155	297	354	801	239
Borivali East	400066	340	550	390	321	127
Kandivali West	400067	437	286	909	126	225

Dahisar	400068	108	57	68	43	31
Andheri East	400069	9	87	412	18	15
Kurla West	400070	2	2	3	11	23
Chembur	400071	80	267	356	180	389
Saki Naka-Chandivali	400072	305	410	78	202	291
Mahul	400074	19	1	130	353	-
Ghatkopar East	400075	306	264	31	136	15
Powai	400076	128	358	321	20	31
Ghatkopar East	400077	212	366	213	696	155
Bhandup West	400078	9	22	75	855	67
Vikhroli	400079	-	7	260	323	-
Mulund West	400080	150	1,231	531	787	330
Mulund East	400081	394	136	157	333	77
Vikhroli	400083	48	88	133	124	46
Ghatkopar West	400086	42	21	108	164	42
Deonar-Mankhurd	400088	255	49	111	53	20
Lokmanya Tilak Terminus	400089	15	363	14	55	147
Borivali West	400091	24	42	108	324	186
Borivali West-Gorai	400092	350	555	528	667	270
Andheri East-Chakala	400093	8	28	26	25	33
Malvani-Marve	400095	70	87	1	-	-
Malad East	400097	121	30	77	68	31
Santacruz East	400098	16	7	83	-	32
Mumbai Airport	400099	-	5	6	28	5
Kandivali East	400101	191	323	68	917	327
Jogeshwari West-Oshiwara	400102	6	45	85	209	739
Mandapeshwar	400103	6	273	93	129	54
Motilal Nagar	400104	298	112	173	154	79
TOTAL		**5,908**	**11,997**	**9,472**	**11,770**	**7,963**

Total New Supply over the years (Offices)						
New Supply in selected micro markets	**Pin Code**	**CY 2021**	**CY 2022**	**CY 2023**	**CY 2024**	**CY 2025**
Kalbadevi	400002	-	5	-	-	-
Girgaon	400004	-	-	19	7	77
Mumbai Central	400008	-	-	18	17	3
Mazgaon Dock	400010	-	1	-	-	-
Byculla West	400011	-	-	12	17	43
Parel	400012	-	16	-	6	-
Lower Parel	400013	72	128	-	1	-
Dadar East	400014	-	-	-	2	9
Mahim/Matunga West	400016	1	1	-	3	187
Matunga	400019	-	-	13	-	-
Sion	400022	3	4	80	219	2
Kurla East	400024	5	-	17	2	-
Prabhadevi	400025	-	-	-	-	28
Dadar West	400028	3	31	-	28	6
Wadala	400031	-	-	-	-	-
Cotton Green	400033	-	1	-	-	-
Antop Hill	400037	-	-	-	-	-
Bhandup East	400042	-	248	4	-	-
Deonar/Govandi West	400043	-	-	-	-	76
Juhu	400049	-	-	-	-	-
Bandra West	400050	-	125	210	2	76
Bandra East	400051	-	1	221	-	245
Khar West	400052	1	119	16	141	2
Andheri-Azad Nagar	400053	191	165	4	-	9
Santacruz West	400054	38	99	27	4	14
Santacruz East	400055	2	-	1	18	173
Vile Parle West	400056	1	-	9	33	3
Vile Parle East	400057	-	80	13	28	3
Andheri West	400058	27	22	91	28	21
Andheri East-Marol	400059	20	3	145	518	52
Jogeshwari East	400060	4	3	264	-	-
Madh-Versova	400061	-	-	-	-	-
Goregaon West	400062	43	-	-	-	-
Goregaon East	400063	321	388	130	423	348
Malad West	400064	3	319	213	381	259
Borivali East	400066	25	830	352	8	164
Kandivali West	400067	235	212	214	365	74

Dahisar	400068	19	215	-	67	122
Andheri East	400069	31	3	50	10	81
Kurla West	400070	1	-	1	3	13
Chembur	400071	20	60	7	95	40
Saki Naka-Chandivali	400072	-	121	-	-	157
Mahul	400074	-	-	-	-	-
Ghatkopar East	400075	-	179	68	4	73
Powai	400076	-	-	-	17	2
Ghatkopar East	400077	246	1	146	156	256
Bhandup West	400078	41	37	107	158	1
Vikhroli	400079	-	715	-	-	-
Mulund West	400080	6	471	721	50	127
Mulund East	400081	8	-	1	5	40
Vikhroli	400083	14	46	21	226	4
Ghatkopar West	400086	319	154	444	138	17
Deonar-Mankhurd	400088	79	3	5	-	-
Lokmanya Tilak Terminus	400089	-	2	-	10	89
Borivali West	400091	8	-	70	62	26
Borivali West-Gorai	400092	205	430	186	393	41
Andheri East-Chakala	400093	242	63	53	82	-
Malvani-Marve	400095	-	10	6	8	3
Malad East	400097	149	14	294	862	7
Santacruz East	400098	-	-	116	165	-
Mumbai Airport	400099	-	28	-	-	-
Kandivali East	400101	40	2	42	-	-
Jogeshwari West-Oshiwara	400102	18	56	315	7	30
Mandapeshwar	400103	-	9	3	16	27
Motilal Nagar	400104	113	17	7	18	1
TOTAL		**2,554**	**5,437**	**4,736**	**4,803**	**3,031**

Total New Supply over the years (Shops)						
New Supply in selected micro markets	Pin Code	CY 2021	CY 2022	CY 2023	CY 2024	CY 2025
Kalbadevi	400002	2	-	9	-	5
Girgaon	400004	4	68	69	57	16
Mumbai Central	400008	28	25	49	69	67
Mazgaon Dock	400010	-	4	40	3	21
Byculla West	400011	20	-	10	32	57
Parel	400012	8	-	10	59	6
Lower Parel	400013	213	31	-	20	7
Dadar East	400014	-	-	24	24	25
Mahim/Matunga West	400016	24	66	4	9	44
Matunga	400019	17	24	14	4	32
Sion	400022	18	26	14	47	31
Kurla East	400024	15	7	12	56	7
Prabhadevi	400025	-	-	-	-	-
Dadar West	400028	21	36	-	37	1
Wadala	400031	61	2	9	-	-
Cotton Green	400033	-	1	-	2	2
Antop Hill	400037	-	18	7	-	16
Bhandup East	400042	41	83	57	13	-
Deonar/Govandi West	400043	26	-	-	-	12
Juhu	400049	-	-	1	-	9
Bandra West	400050	70	16	10	27	56
Bandra East	400051	3	69	72	10	5
Khar West	400052	-	14	9	10	8
Andheri-Azad Nagar	400053	41	28	52	21	33
Santacruz West	400054	1	23	13	30	13
Santacruz East	400055	16	9	34	11	29
Vile Parle West	400056	4	-	47	27	20
Vile Parle East	400057	10	52	57	68	21
Andheri West	400058	63	11	10	39	35
Andheri East-Marol	400059	70	10	18	20	15
Jogeshwari East	400060	6	217	51	1	9
Madh-Versova	400061	-	-	-	-	20
Goregaon West	400062	11	15	2	-	29
Goregaon East	400063	11	9	12	78	138
Malad West	400064	176	38	87	191	147
Borivali East	400066	35	113	111	136	106
Kandivali West	400067	79	166	229	228	158

Dahisar	400068	52	150	21	70	71
Andheri East	400069	9	19	95	15	8
Kurla West	400070	4	11	9	35	10
Chembur	400071	48	64	125	59	51
Saki Naka-Chandivali	400072	108	27	19	44	103
Mahul	400074	5	-	23	39	8
Ghatkopar East	400075	45	16	22	21	34
Powai	400076	-	2	9	8	1
Ghatkopar East	400077	47	15	54	82	59
Bhandup West	400078	76	49	111	147	66
Vikhroli	400079	-	5	-	7	-
Mulund West	400080	21	75	112	131	119
Mulund East	400081	28	27	32	41	53
Vikhroli	400083	85	108	156	55	35
Ghatkopar West	400086	18	39	46	34	28
Deonar-Mankhurd	400088	5	6	8	28	-
Lokmanya Tilak Terminus	400089	8	43	-	36	14
Borivali West	400091	10	9	26	30	50
Borivali West-Gorai	400092	136	167	160	264	212
Andheri East-Chakala	400093	115	13	10	-	9
Malvani-Marve	400095	5	54	44	26	4
Malad East	400097	21	242	116	107	42
Santacruz East	400098	4	-	3	1	2
Mumbai Airport	400099	-	9	-	10	8
Kandivali East	400101	13	8	18	43	113
Jogeshwari West-Oshiwara	400102	25	50	75	86	168
Mandapeshwar	400103	-	54	28	82	53
Motilal Nagar	400104	80	181	16	68	27
TOTAL		**2,062**	**2,624**	**2,481**	**2,898**	**2,548**

www.ingramcontent.com/pod-product-compliance
Lightning Source LLC
LaVergne TN
LVHW070936210926
848482LV00003B/256